50 SKETCHES ABOUT JESUS

For Dad

50 Sketches
About Jesus

DAVID BURT

EASTBOURNE

ISBN 0 85476 814 9

Published by
KINGSWAY COMMUNICATIONS LTD
Lottbridge Drove, Eastbourne, BN23 6NT, England.
Email: books@kingsway.co.uk

Book design and production for the publishers by
Bookprint Creative Services, P.O. Box 827, BN21 3YJ, England.
Printed in Great Britain.

Contents

Performance and Copyright

The right to perform sketches in this book is included in the price, provided that such performances are made within an amateur context, for example worship or education. Where any charge is made to audiences, permission in writing must be obtained from the author, who can be contacted care of the publisher, and a fee may be payable for the right to do this.

Please note that the text of this book is copyright, and that no part may be copied without permission in writing from the publisher. Where multiple copies of a sketch are required for those playing the parts, it is generally simpler and cheaper to buy extra copies of the book.

Acknowledgements

My most sincere thanks are owed to the following people for their help and support towards the production of this book.

First, a huge thank you to all my family and friends who remain so encouraging, and often unknowingly give me ideas for characters and situations. I warn you now, you may find yourselves, albeit disguised, in the following pages!

Thanks to Richard Herkes and the team at Kingsway for their support. I hope we get to do it again sometime. For advice and the inspiration to get my creative juices flowing, I thank Paul Burbridge and the mob at Riding Lights Theatre Company. I look forward to seeing you all again very soon.

For my new family of friends at Soapbox Communications, I give my appreciation and respect, in particular to Steve Flashman for his boundless insight and enthusiasm.

I also owe a debt of gratitude to all the people who have at various stages 'guinea pigged' the material in this book. My particular thanks go to Tom Richardson and Bare Witness Theatre Company at Durham University.

Finally, a big thank you to David James for his invaluable help with the manuscript. I hope all the brackets and italics didn't give you too many sleepless nights!

If I've missed anyone else out . . . oops, sorry!

God bless you all.

Dave Burt

Preface

With the new millennium dawning, a book of sketches about Jesus is well-timed to help us understand the man who is quite literally right at the centre of BC and AD. At this key point in our history, many people are asking questions about the origins of the calendar, and so about Jesus, the man by whose birth and death we date everything in the past, present and future.

Using drama we can communicate the life and teachings of Jesus in an entertaining, challenging and often humorous way. Regardless of age, size of group, level of ability or intended audience, there should be something in this jamboree bag suitable for your needs. If you feel there is an important area I've left out, drop me a line care of the publisher, and, who knows, there may be a volume two!

David Burt

Before You Begin

My aim in this part of the book is not to give rigid 'how-to' instructions, but rather to give some suggestions – more like an ideas factory – where the reader or listener will pick up some good tips but also dispense with anything not applicable to their situation.

The Use of Drama

Defending the use of drama in the communication of a Christian message may seem faintly odd in these pages, as it's fairly obvious that anyone purchasing this book is already sold on the idea. However, you may find this useful, as over the years the church has had a bit of a stormy relationship with the arts.

Nowadays, most of the church is open to the use of many creative art forms as part of its life and worship, but in the late sixties and seventies, it was a rather different story. As a result of the drug-induced music scene, a wave of dubious films being banned and the theatre becoming increasingly erotic, the church seemed to distance itself from any possible connection with the arts. Strumming a guitar was about as daring as it got, and the suggestion of using drama as part of worship would have been greeted in many quarters with gasps of outrage and calls for repentance!

My pastor became a Christian in the early seventies at about the same time as he was applying to various drama schools in London. He was offered places at a couple of very good schools, but the pressure from his new Christian friends eventually caused him to reject his offers. The terrifying end to this story is that the poor guy ultimately became a minister (only joking Pete!). This story perfectly illustrates the strained and uneasy relationship between the church and the arts at that time.

The central defence for using drama to communicate biblical truth is simply that the Bible is very dramatic. I am totally convinced that anyone who says that the Bible is boring has in all honesty never actually read it – unless the only bits they've come across are the genealogies. It's got the lot: love, war, peace, betrayal, miracles, violence, sex, murder and a message of hope – though not necessarily in that order. There's so much in it that when Hollywood attempts to make a film about it, they can only cover a few chapters at a time and the films last for about six and a half hours. If you look at a lot of stories, particularly in the Old Testament, they make Quentin Tarantino's *Pulp Fiction* look like a bedtime story! The Bible *is* dramatic: our challenge is to present it in a way that will make people sit up and listen.

Advertisers plunge to whatever depths are necessary to package their products in a way that will make them irresistible to the consumer. 'Unless you buy our revitalising shampoo with added vitamins, minerals and essence of jojoba, your hair will be an unconditioned, greasy and dandruff-infested disaster area . . .' They, of course, are usually peddling lies, whereas we have an exciting and life-changing truth to share. How much more important, then, that we communicate it effectively.

If to do this we need to follow an example, we need look no further than Jesus himself. He recognised the value of engaging his listeners, and we see him doing this countless times in his method of speaking and, of course, supremely through his parables. By letting people listen to and watch drama (and maybe even take part), we involve more of their senses, so the message goes in at different levels. It is not simply heard, but also understood.

Who's it for and why?

We've established that drama is a good way of communicating the gospel, but we shouldn't just perform for the sake of it. We need to know *why* we are performing a particular piece. Always decide your objective before staging any piece of drama, as this will dictate which sketch you select. Is it to bring a biblical story to life, to illustrate a particular kind of behaviour and its consequences, or to challenge the audience's response to the gospel? There can be dozens of reasons like these to use drama, but we should be able to sum up in a sentence what our objective is in using it.

We must also consider who our audience will be. This may seem obvious, but many times groups put together a piece, often brilliantly, but it is totally inappropriate to the audience or setting. Always check the age and knowledge of Scripture of who you will be performing to before selecting which piece to do. The setting is also important; for instance, one piece may be perfect for a raucous youth event but not for a communion service! It's all common sense really, but absolutely vital that you get this right if you want to achieve maximum impact.

Words of warning

I don't wish to appear a gloom-monger, but as well as establishing who you're performing to and why, I have one little word of warning. However good a piece of writing may be, there is no such thing as an actor- or director-proof sketch. In other words, even with a complete script in front of you, there is still a lot of work to do. I'm sure we've all sat through some dire productions of Shakespeare plays, and we can hardly blame the bard himself for these disasters. A collection of sketches such as these here can only be a resource book; the success of the piece rests essentially with the group who put it together.

Be encouraged, though! God has made us creative beings, and I've seen some fantastic pieces of drama put together by groups with no professional training, just a love and an

interest in using drama to serve God. Do your homework,
be enthusiastic and go for it!

How to use this book

You're ready to do some drama, and now you want to choose
an appropriate sketch. There are various features of this
book which should assist that selection process.

The material has been grouped under four main sections
according to content: 'Meet Jesus' (his ministry, death and
resurrection, impact on history); 'Walk the Talk' (aspects of
the Christian life and lifestyle); 'Reaching Out' (sketches
which could be used evangelistically) and 'Christmas Is
Coming'. Some sketches can obviously 'transfer' across
these categories (e.g. some in 'Meet Jesus' could be used in
evangelism), so can be used in different contexts.

For easy reference, there is also a detailed index, sub-
divided into different sections. There is one index for types
of sketches, one for subjects and another for Bible references. By using these, you can see quickly which of the
sketches are most likely to suit your requirements.
Unfortunately, however long an index is, it can never be
totally exhaustive. So, if you have time, the best way to
choose a sketch is to get a cup of coffee, sit down and read
through the book, thinking of your potential actors and
audience, and defining your objectives.

As an additional guideline, each sketch also has a teaching point listed, plus the appropriate Bible reference where
the story or teaching can be found. It is my belief that,
however important drama is, it does not in any way, shape or
form replace the Bible, but rather serves it by causing people
to look back at the Scriptures again. The reference which
accompanies the sketch will be especially useful if you need
a drama to link in with some form of teaching on a specific
passage.

And finally . . .

Unless you are performing a full-length play (none included here, I'm afraid), your dramatic offering will more than likely form part of a larger presentation – whether that is a church service, youth group discussion, outreach evening or whatever. A sketch will have maximum effect if *everyone* involved in that wider programme knows its content and objective. There is no point 'doing drama because trendy churches do it' – that's a sure-fire way to get it dropped from your church's agenda because people won't see the point of it. A dramatic piece needs to contribute to the overall message, to be built upon and referred to, but not over-explained or done to death!

Types of Sketches

The sketches in this book can be split into eight types or styles, some of which fall into more than one category. I have listed these below, with a few suggestions as to how they might be used. I have also used these headings in the index at the back of the book, so you can easily find sketches appropriate to your situation.

Monologues

A common misconception about the monologue is that it's the easiest and quickest style of sketch to put together. Of course, rehearsal is made easier by not having to find times when all the cast can meet, but it's probably the most difficult to actually perform. Only a competent actor should attempt the monologue; it is certainly not a suitable starting-point for a beginner. Remember, if you forget your lines or start to sink, you're on your own!

When rehearsing a monologue, always speak the lines out loud, as if you were performing the piece. Running through the lines in your head or muttering them under your breath is a totally different thing from speaking them out loud. Also, use another person to work with you as a director; they can give you advice and will notice things that you may never see practising for hours in front of a mirror.

The confessional style that most monologues adopt allows us to peel back the known facts about a character and really get under their skin, to understand how they feel. In my opinion, a well-put-together monologue can be one of the most powerful, thought-provoking styles of drama.

Two-handers

When writing this book, I was very aware that in many churches very few people have a gift in the area of drama. I therefore decided to make a large number of the sketches for two performers. If you are in a situation where maybe just a couple of you have talent and enjoy drama, most pastors would be very keen to use your abilities in the services.

Rehearsal is fairly easy with only two people, plus, if possible, another person as a director. If there really is no one else, decide on one person to be overall director, obviously listening to input from the second person. Many of the two-handers in the book, although initially gender-specific, can easily be converted by changing names and the odd line to suit your ratio of performers. For instance, *The Calendar System* is written for one man and one woman, but could easily be changed to suit two men or two women.

Narrated

I have spoken to lots of people about the kind of material they would be most likely to use in a drama resource book, and narrated pieces proved highly popular. The beauty of them is that they can be put together without anybody having to go through the odious task of learning lines – a major stumbling-block for many when considering using drama. They are also ideal for use with children, or for occasions when time is very much against you and a piece has to be put together quickly. They can also stretch a group's creative muscles during rehearsal, as they try to come up with funny and original ideas to act out the script. (How would you do actions for the fruit of the Spirit in *Who Am I?*) Audiences love them, and they can still be used by groups whose ability may not be as strong as others.

As an alternative to one person reading the narration, a more confident group could all create the actions and divide the text between them. With plenty of rehearsal, a narrated piece performed in this way can look really slick and professional.

Raps and rhymes

I have included a few raps and rhymes in the book, as they are a very popular and effective sketch form. Although they do not necessarily require the greatest actors, the obvious disadvantage is that they will inevitably involve lengthy periods of rehearsal. When the pieces are used with lots of movement, it can be quite a discipline to keep rhythm while remembering lines and choreography.

However, I do not want to paint a gloomy picture. The disadvantages are far outweighed by the impressive end product. If you have plenty of rehearsal time and decide that a rap or rhyme would best suit your intended audience, I really encourage you to persevere. Learning a rhythm piece can be like learning how to drive. You understand steering, clutch control and gear changes, but somehow it still doesn't make sense; then, all of a sudden, something clicks and it all falls into place. It can be like this with a rhythm sketch. During rehearsal, the piece can often look a complete shambles, but with perseverance, you will achieve a breakthrough and the end result will be well worth all the hard work.

Encouraging creativity

When writing sketches, it can be difficult to know how much detail to give with regard to stage direction. Do you literally specify every movement (SARAH takes two steps forward), or do you give none at all and leave it up to the director and actors to work them out? Some groups prefer to be spoon-fed; others like the flexibility to stretch their creative muscles.

Many of the sketches in this book have been written particularly to encourage a group's creativity. That doesn't mean they are always the hardest to put together and perform, but they should allow your group to stamp their individuality on the piece. I have led workshops in the past where members of the group have had a very low opinion of their abilities, but after using various exercises to encourage their creativity, the results have been simply fantastic! I believe we have God-given creativity; we just need to give it a chance to shine through.

Suitable for children

Using drama with children can sometimes lead to a performance, but it can also be used purely as a learn-by-doing exercise. (See the section entitled 'Something for the Kids'.) If you plan to perform a piece, prepare well and allow lots of rehearsal time; if you've avoided using drama with your children because of the work involved in producing a finished product, be encouraged to use it as a learning tool. It can be lots of fun and you may spot a budding Robert de Niro!

Prior knowledge needed

It is important when selecting a sketch to perform that you make sure it is suitable for the audience. Although it's extremely 'arty' and 'cultural' to go to the theatre to see a Pinter play and come out not having a clue what it was all about, when communicating the gospel, it is imperative that our audience understands the message.

Certain sketches in this book do require some prior

knowledge of the Bible stories they are based on, and this needs to be carefully considered before performing them. For instance, if you perform *Hole in the Roof* to an audience which isn't familiar with the miracle of the paralysed man lowered through the roof to be healed by Jesus, the sketch's central joke will be totally lost on them!

Suitable for schools

In a school it is often best to perform a punchy, funny piece, but we also need to ensure that we communicate the thrust of the gospel. The vast majority of sketches in this book could be used in a school, depending on the age group, but some will obviously work better than others.

Remember, if you are performing a piece in an assembly, it must stand totally on its own, without any explanation. If you are taking a lesson, you can perform a few sketches, then discuss some issues raised to make sure that your message has been understood.

Topicality

One of the joys of using drama is that the material can be very contemporary, enabling the audience to relate to it easily. This obviously has its downside, in that sketches can 'go past their sell-by date' quite quickly. References to chart-topping bands, Hollywood mega-stars or headline news stories need vigilant updating. Throughout this book, therefore, I have indicated such instances with an asterisk and footnote; the necessary adaptations I leave to your own creative instincts!

Something for the Kids

When I had the privilege of running seminars and work-shops at the Kingsway Children's Ministry Conferences on using drama with children, the response was encouraging, so it is worth noting some of the key points here.

With children, the main reason to use drama is often not to perform, but to inform as they learn by actually doing. If you decide to use drama in a session with your children, it's always good to plan the whole session ahead of time. Here are some suggestions for a typical evening:

Warm-up

Begin by doing a mini-physical workout with them – some-thing which is fun, but not too strenuous. As well as warming them up physically, do some facial workouts, e.g. opening the face as wide as possible, then scrunching it up as tight as possible, pretend to chew large and sticky toffees, and do horse-blows to limber up the lips. (The children will abso-lutely love all this!) Finally, a basic vocal warm-up is advis-able; repeating some famous tongue-twisters is a good way to do this.

Games

After a warm-up, it's good fun to play a game or two. No

particular style is necessary – you can use any good games that you know which involve a mixture of energetic dashing around and basic concentration.

Mini-drama exercises

Now you can move on to some exercises more directly related to drama skills.

Machines

Split the children into two groups and give them a few minutes to act out a machine of their own choosing, including its features, movements and noises. A little tip when using this exercise is to ban them from using a television; in my experience, about 60 per cent of children choose this and it can get a bit boring!

Character walks

Get the children to move their bodies on the spot, bending knees, leaning over and backwards, etc. When the leader shouts 'Freeze', they must hold their final position for ten seconds, then start to walk holding that pose. From this, they start to develop a character. As they walk around in silence, let them think about the character's name, age, job, hobbies, where they are going, etc. If you have time, spotlight a few of them and get the rest of the group to ask them questions while they stay in character. If this sounds a bit advanced for your children, be assured that, regardless of age, kids are absolutely brilliant at it!

Emotional freeze frames

Split the children into groups again, and give each of them an emotion, e.g. love, anger, grief, fear. In just a few minutes, they must come up with a freeze-frame illustrating that emotion. This can take the form of a realistic scene, or alternatively, a more surreal image suggesting that emotion. The groups then try and guess each other's emotions. Again, this exercise is very short and great fun, but more importantly it begins to use the children's creative abilities.

Main exercises

All the previous suggestions are a preamble to the central exercise, where you complete your objective to teach whichever story, gospel truth or moral you have selected. There are various methods of doing this.

Use the Bible text

Simply having a person narrate a story from Scripture, and working out actions and noises with the children, is a very basic but fun and effective way of letting the children learn by doing. You can also *narrate from a children's Bible*. These have excellent paraphrased versions of most of the main Bible stories, and can sometimes be easier to use as a narration than the Bible text itself.

Have a go at the creative process yourselves!

This may freak some people out, but start by simply writing your own paraphrases from either the Bible or a children's Bible. You can easily slip humour into the stories by making mention of current issues (England's football results, major news items, the latest gossip from the soap operas), popular celebrities or even people from your own church who are well known to the kids and audience if you are also performing – having made sure they are people with a good sense of humour and no tendencies towards paranoia!

Find suitable sketches

Sketch books are written as a resource, and I hope this one has many suitable sketches that you will be able to use in the course of time. There are lots of other books available with sketches suitable for children and, although scripted pieces may be a bit harder to put together, the end results are worth it.

Improvisations

If there's one word related to drama that scares people off, it's improvisation. Immediately images of *Whose Line Is It Anyway?* leap to mind, and people react by running a mile. Children however, with their natural lack of inhibition, love it! Decide on the story you want to work on, and get groups to improvise various scenes based on it. One of my favourites is to use verses from Proverbs: Proverbs 11:13, for example, speaks about gossiping, and you can get a group to improvise around this passage set in a doctor's surgery, at a bus stop or even in church!

Whichever style of drama you choose to use with children, always end your session with a question time to check what they have learnt, and to see if your objective has been achieved. If you've worked on a drama based on the story of Noah, ask the child playing Noah how they felt when the neighbours made fun of his strange hobby. Hopefully, they will not just have had fun doing the drama, but have inwardly digested the various lessons through the stories too.

Drama Groups

Many churches don't have drama groups, either because they are too small or because not enough people have the desire or talent to join one. I believe that the most successful drama groups are built on quality and not quantity of members, and with this in mind, may I draw your attention to Jesus' famous words: 'Where two or three come together in my name, there am I with them' (Matthew 18:20). Now I know this is slightly out of context, but the same principle applies! Obviously not everyone has a gift in the area of drama, but if there are just two or three people in your church with interest and talent, you have enough people to start a drama group. Over a third of the sketches in this book are two-handers. So, be encouraged. Get together, ask your leaders for support in what you want to do and then just go for it! Once you get up and running, other people may want to join in, but if not, don't panic. Just carry on in your small group and work on being a real blessing to everyone else using your God-given abilities.

However, I believe it is a fallacy that anyone, regardless of ability, should be allowed to join a drama group and perform in church. This may seem harsh and rather discouraging, but actually it is perfectly reasonable. I would absolutely love to be in the band at church, looking cool and trendy strumming a guitar, tickling the ivories or, best of all, whacking the drums. But in the musical department, I'm totally inept, and the worship leader would – in a lovely Christian way, of course – refuse my request to join the band. Why then do people think that anybody, regardless of ability, can join a drama group? Don't misunderstand me: I strongly believe drama is for everyone, and people with talent can run workshops and help those who purely enjoy it. But if you are running a *drama group*, don't feel obliged to let everyone join and be in your productions, purely because they fancy themselves as the new Pacino.

Two of the major problems in the church today are first, people with wonderful gifts who are either too scared to use them or haven't yet discovered them, and second, people who think they have a particular gift which they quite clearly haven't! That may sound somewhat harsh, but the crucial truth to grasp is that every single person *does have gifts*; we need to make sure that we all discover them and then use them for God's glory in the areas we have been given them.

How to Get Laughs

If someone could concoct a formula to guarantee laughter, they would become a millionaire overnight. Unfortunately, it's not quite that easy. One person may find something hilarious, while another will look on with a vacant stare. Some performers have a special gift for creating laughter, having to do seemingly little to cause hysteria, while others have to work really hard to drum up a few sniggers. Tommy Cooper, who certainly had a natural ability to create laughter, only had to walk on stage and his audience would be in convulsions. For most, though, it's not like that. Put simply, getting laughs is no laughing matter!

So, if comedy is a natural ability bestowed on a few, how can other people gain those elusive laughs? Well, nothing of course can replace natural ability and lots of experience, but there are some areas where laughs can be found . . . or indeed lost!

Comic timing

We hear about it so often, and it is at the very centre of truly great comic performances, but what is it? Above all, comic timing is a skill you learn as you gain more experience in front of audiences. It is the sixth sense of delivering the line not too early, but not too late, for maximum impact. Never deliver a line while the audience are still laughing, as they will miss what you have said. But don't wait until all the laughter has stopped, leaving an awkward silence, as this will kill off the pace and momentum. In effect, you should deliver the line just at the moment when the laughter is dying down but hasn't actually finished.

It's difficult to explain any further without becoming too formulaic, but I encourage you to watch live performances or recordings of comedy, and watch for the timing and its power to control the laughter.

Milking the cow

When a performer knows they have a funny line, they have fallen into a potential minefield if they are tempted to 'milk the line'. Milking is basically giving far too much emphasis to a line, when in actual fact, saying the line naturally will always be the funniest. Performers who do this are quite simply selfish! They spend the minute leading up to the line preparing to forcibly thrust the witticism on the audience, and in the process kill what the ensemble cast has been collectively trying to achieve.

The best although rather generalised advice I can give, is to keep your performance deadpan. As soon as you start looking smug and thinking that you're incredibly funny, you're not! A good way to stop any potential 'milkers' in their tracks, is to have a discipline in rehearsal, whereby when anyone starts to milk a line, the rest of the cast mime the action of milking a cow. This will usually embarrass the guilty party into stopping, and it's also great fun!

Creating a character

Strong characterisations are a key ingredient for any good performance, particularly in comedy, and the funniest characters are the ones that are the most believable. If you are interested in drama, one of the best things you can do is to observe people's behaviour patterns. I find it fascinating to visit my local Asda supermarket, buy a cappuccino in the café, and then to watch the hundreds of people going by, taking in all their individual movements, speech and nuances. An hour of this can provide a cauldron of ideas for characters.

I have been criticised in my time for rather over-the-top caricature performances, and while in a full-length play they can be unsuitable, for short sketches such as the ones in this book, I believe there can be a place for them. With a caricature performance there are no subtleties. What you see is what you get, and in a five-minute sketch, where there is no time for character development, this can be beneficial.

However you play a character, though, it must have a degree of believability, and in rehearsal it is good to play around with characters, spotlighting each other and asking questions to help give them a bit more depth. From this, the actor can make any necessary tweaks. Again, researching the great comic performers for tips is wise, and for characterisation you would be hard pushed to better Peter Sellers.

What to use and where to put it!

Staging and props are often overlooked, but careful attention to how to stage a piece and a few well-chosen props can create laughter before a line is even spoken. I'm not talking about elaborate set design, revolving stages and numerous costume changes, but simply a few basic touches. For instance, in a sketch with fishermen or thieves, put some thought into costumes: use wellie boots, huge jackets and funny hats or stripey tops, swag-bags and balaclavas. A few props appropriate to the sketch are worthwhile, and they can also be quite funny – just imagine Pontius Pilate sitting at his desk playing with a child's wind-up toy!

The staging of a piece can also be crucial to its impact. Carefully consider where the audience will be, and place any props and furniture in the best position. This is especially important in a sketch which involves the cast sitting down to deliver lines.

Good script and direction

When an actor collects an award for best performance, how often does he or she pay tribute to the writer and director? Admittedly, this can be false modesty, as the actor has obviously had an influential part to play, but I believe that good comedy is very much a team effort – a mixture of performance, script and direction.

Personal taste naturally dictates what will make any individual laugh but, when looking for a comedy script, use one the group collectively finds funny. It's very important that you perform a piece that you all believe in. If the cast are quite simply bored or disillusioned with the piece they are performing, it makes for very stale viewing.

Good direction is also a key element in comedy. The director should preferably be someone who is not actually performing, but who has a good eye for what works on stage. They have a much better overall view of the piece by standing on the outside, and should be able to pick up on any humour which is simply not working. They should also direct when the pace of a piece needs to pick up.

The laughter of recognition

A very popular ingredient of successful comedy is to create laughter by recognition, commonly known as observational humour. This style is very much associated with stand-up comedy, but can also be employed in sketches. It requires the performer to devise a situation which the audience can immediately identify with. This can be an habitual human foible, a common and frustrating bureaucratic circumstance or just something that generally tends to happen to us all in life.

For instance, in a supermarket, whichever queue you choose, the next one seems to move faster and the person in front of you is always paying by cheque! Human beings also have a strange tendency to think that if you pick your nose in the privacy of your car while in a traffic queue, no one else in the world can see you! And on the subject of noses, why do we get to a certain age, then suddenly sprout nasal hair?

These may seem like silly examples, but they provide fertile ground for dramatic comedy. Think about funny things that happen to you in life, and the chances are they happen to lots of other people too.

What's that doing there?

Another useful tip for getting that much-hankered-after guffaw is to have something or someone which is totally out of place, or a little bit surreal. This is not an astoundingly original suggestion, but it still gets laughs!

A few examples you will come across in this volume are: Zacchaeus communicating with a talking tree, Jesus preaching at Wembley Stadium, a paparazzi photographer in Bethlehem, Bible characters discussing the Spice Girls, Mary cooking spaghetti hoops on toast, the wise men shopping in Harrods, Joseph registering Jesus' birth at the town hall, and Burger King restaurants in heaven. All ridiculous, I admit, but bizarre and incongruous situations can work very well when creating a humorous sketch.

In Your Own Write?

I would like to give any budding writers the encouragement to pick up their pens and have a go at scripting some sketches themselves. Unfortunately, a talent for good writing is something that some people possess and some don't, but you won't know until you put pen to paper and have a try.

Be warned that it can be a very slow process. Sometimes the ideas are free-flowing and you can't write fast enough, but at other times, it can be a real slog and you have to be very disciplined. Also, don't expect to get it right first time: my notebook is covered in huge crossings-out and scribbles.

Getting your ideas needn't be a hard task, it can actually be great fun. Go and see as many plays as you can, read lots of good books and keep your eyes open for current issues in the newspapers. I'm not proposing that you plagiarise someone else's work, but taking in as many creative forms as possible will give you ideas for suitable content and styles that will work when employed on the stage.

Always think of your 'target-audience' when writing: are you aiming at 'clued-up' Christians, or fringe people, or seekers, or the totally unchurched? Make sure you use language and situations which will be familiar and accessible.

You will also need to be willing to take some criticism from other people. I have been fortunate to have a group who have 'guinea-pigged' some of the sketches in this book, and they give me encouragement for things that really work, but also tell me (quite bluntly!) if something is a non-starter. I admit this can be tough when you've put hours of graft into something, but we need to realise that there are times when a situation that seems stupendously funny as you write at your desk can be a lame duck when actually put onto the stage. Find someone whose opinion you value, who will be constructive in their criticism, and make a vow not to get too over-defensive when at times they disagree with you.

PART 2

The Sketches

Meet Jesus

(A) MIRACLES

Dirty Water

INTRODUCTION

In this sketch we see Jesus' first public miracle, changing the water into wine, from the point of view of two wine waitresses and a wine waiter. The characters have been written for strong caricature performances, and if possible are best played with a strong Liverpool accent.

Characters: MARIE; JEANETTE; KEV.

MARIE and JEANETTE are on their tea break from work. We join them mid conversation.

MARIE:	My favourite telly programme's on tonight.
JEANETTE:	What's that, love?
MARIE:	*The Des O'Connor Show*. Did you see it last week?
JEANETTE:	Ooh yeah, I never miss it. He's absolutely gorgeous.
MARIE:	He is, isn't he? Lovely looking, especially when you consider he's dead old.
JEANETTE:	Yeah, he must be well into his fifties.
MARIE:	And I'll tell you what. I think that tan's for real and all.
JEANETTE:	Oh, I think you're right there, Marie. If it were one of them fake ones, it would start running under all those studio lights.
MARIE:	I'll tell you whose is fake though. That other one.

JEANETTE:	Who do you mean, love?
MARIE:	Oh, what's his name? The horrible smarmy one . . . Bob Monkhouse!
JEANETTE:	Ugghhh yeah! He's gross, isn't he?
MARIE:	Terrible. And there's no way on God's earth his tan isn't out of a bottle!
JEANETTE:	I agree with you there too, love. Given the choice of Des or Bob, I'd go with Des anytime. (*KEV enters*)
KEV:	Oh, it's my lucky day. The two most gorgeous wine waitresses in Galilee!
MARIE:	Mind out, Jeanette love, here comes roaming-hands Romeo.
KEV:	(*Tries to cuddle girls*) And how's my two lovely Juliets today?
MARIE:	Hey you! Watch the hands right, or we'll have you done for sexual harassment in the workplace!
KEV:	Charming! There's a nice welcome when I've come all the way up here to give you ladies some good news.
MARIE:	Well, I could do with some of that. This wedding's been going on for five days now, and I'm absolutely shattered.
JEANETTE:	Yeah, me too. Come on, Kevin love, what's this good news?
KEV:	Is it worth a little peck on the cheek from both of you?
MARIE:	No! And if you don't tell us in the next five seconds, I'll be forced to stick this corkscrew somewhere that'll make you scream.
KEV:	(*Backing off*) All right, all right! There's no need to resort to violence. I just thought you might like to know that the wine's nearly run out.

JEANETTE: You're joking!

KEV: No, everything's gone except half a dozen bottles of Lambrusco and a crate of Blue Nun.

MARIE: I like the way they've left all the vinegar till the end.

JEANETTE: This is fantastic! If they run out of wine, they won't need any wine waitresses.

MARIE: If they run out of wine, love, the guests will be gone so fast, you won't see 'em for dust!

KEV: Whichever way you look at it, girls, we'll be getting off early.

MARIE: Right Kev, you check them last few bottles of plonk have gone, and we'll get our bags ready.

KEV: Righto! (*KEV exits*)

MARIE: Oh, this is great! I might give my John a ring, and get him to knock me up a fry-up for when I get in.

JEANETTE: That wine running out is gonna be a terrible embarrassment for the bride's parents, isn't it, Marie?

MARIE: (*Pretending to feel sorry*) Oh, it is Jeanette. A terrible shame. My heart bleeds. (*They both laugh*) Oh well, the bride's mum was a bit of an old battleaxe anyway.

JEANETTE: Yeah, and did you see the state of that hat she was wearing?

MARIE: Terrible, wasn't it? It looked like a decapitated chicken stuck on her head! (*They both fall into hysterics. KEV then rushes in holding a bottle of coloured water*) All right, Kev love, we're all ready.

KEV: We've got a slight problem with the water.

MARIE: Yuk! It looks absolutely filthy!

KEV: Have a taste.

MARIE: What do you think I am? Stupid? It's probably poisonous or something. You taste it, Jeanette.

KEV: Go on, Jeanette. There's nothing wrong with it, honest.

JEANETTE: (*Has a swig*) Oooh! That's fantastic. Best we've pinched all evening. Go on, Marie.

MARIE: (*Has a swig*) Ooh, you're not wrong there, Jeanette. That's good stuff. What's it doing in a plastic Evian bottle?

KEV: Well, twenty minutes ago, it *was* a bottle of Evian water.

JEANETTE: What are you talking about?

KEV: One of the guests is some kind of miracle-worker, and he's changing water into wine.

MARIE: Water into wine, my foot! It's just an illusion, you big divvy. He's probably got the wine shoved up his sleeve or something.

KEV: I don't think so, Marie. There's a bit too much of it to fit up his sleeve.

JEANETTE: How much 'as he changed then, love?

KEV: About a hundred and twenty gallons.

MARIE: (*Incredulous*) A hundred and twenty gallons?

KEV: Yep, and it's all top quality booze, none of your cheap paint-stripper stuff.

JEANETTE: So I suppose the party's still in full swing?

KEV: Thanks to this guy, more than ever.

MARIE: You know what this means, Jeanette.

JEANETTE: What, love?

MARIE: We'll be missing *The Des O'Connor Show* tonight.

JEANETTE: Oh no! And his special guest tonight is that Nigel Havers, who is absolutely gorgeous.

MARIE: Oh, well, let's get back to work. You can point out this miracle-worker to me, Kev, 'cos I tell ya, I'm gonna swing for him. Come on, you two. (*They all exit, mumbling to each other. Lights fade to blackout*)

TEACHING POINT

Jesus' miracles are not always greeted with universal enthusiasm.

BIBLE REFERENCE

John 2:1–11

Hole in the Roof

INTRODUCTION

This sketch gives an interesting slant on the miracle of the paralysed man, who was healed after his friends lowered him through the roof of a house to meet Jesus. The action takes place the following day, and is seen from the point of view of the landlord and tenant of the property where the event took place.

Characters: LINTON, a landlord; EVANS, his tenant.

LINTON: Good morning, Mr Evans. I understand there's a bit of a structural problem with your rented property.

EVANS: Ah yes, thank you for coming so quickly, Mr Linton. I'm afraid it is rather an urgent problem.

LINTON: Well, let's have a look then. I don't want any of my tenants to suffer any kind of discomfort or inconvenience.

EVANS: Well, basically it's a problem with the, er, the roof. It has rather a large hole. (*He points towards roof*)

LINTON: (*Looks up in shock*) Good grief! Look at the size of it. How on earth did that happen? Was it a natural occurrence – rain, lightning, thunder, gales?

EVANS: Er, no.

LINTON: An unusual flying object?

EVANS: No.

LINTON: Well, I'm going to need more specific details for
my insurance claim, Mr Evans. I mean, that
hole's big enough for a man to come through!

EVANS: Ah! You've hit the nail on the head there, Mr
Linton.

LINTON: What, a man came through? What was it, a
robbery? Oh, they're devious, aren't they? You
lock up your windows and doors, and the blight-
ers smash in through your roof. Honestly, what
will they think of next?

EVANS: Actually, it wasn't a robber as such. It's rather
difficult to explain. You see, he was, in a round-
about kind of way, a guest.

LINTON: A guest! Well, I've heard of dropping in on your
friends and neighbours, but that just about takes
the biscuit.

EVANS: Sorry, I'm not being very clear. Coming through
the roof was not his first option, but he couldn't
physically get in through the door.

LINTON: Ahhh! Explain no more, Mr Evans. I think I've
got it. There's some sort of fault on the lock
mechanism of the door, and you and your
guest had to break in through the roof to gain
entry.

EVANS: No. I was already in, as were a number of other
guests, so entry via the door was blocked.

LINTON: Hang on a minute. What do you mean, entry via
the door was blocked? How many guests did you
have in here exactly?

EVANS: (*Tentatively*) Oh, I don't know exactly. Probably
in the region of a hundred.

LINTON: (*Exploding*) Stone the living crows! A hundred?

EVANS: Or maybe a few more.

LINTON: Gracious, man, you'll have the health and safety
mob down on me like a ton of bricks! Don't you

realise this property is designed to house, at maximum, a family of four?

EVANS: Yes, Mr Linton.

LINTON: Well, what were you playing at? I suppose you were having one of those new-fangled rave things?

EVANS: No, nothing like that, I can assure you.

LINTON: Oh, that's what you say. I don't doubt you had the place full of booze and drugs and floozies.

EVANS: Really, I promise you, nothing could be further from the truth.

LINTON: Well, what were you up to then, with a hundred people, that resulted in there being a whacking great hole in my roof?

EVANS: (*Pause*) Have you heard of this man called Jesus who's travelling around teaching and healing at the moment?

LINTON: Oh yeah, the wife caught his Sermon on the Mount the other day. Said it was very good.

EVANS: Yes, well, I invited him round to speak to a group of my friends and, well, things got a bit out of hand. Soon the place was teeming with people and I was powerless to stop it.

LINTON: Yeah, carry on.

EVANS: Well, unbeknown to me a paralysed man had been brought by his friends to see Jesus, but of course by the time they arrived the house was chocka, and there was no way through the door. So they . . .

LINTON: (*Interrupts*) I think I've got it. They took him up on the roof, removed my lovely tiles and bunged him down that way.

EVANS: Basically, yeah.

LINTON: So what happened next then?

EVANS: Well, I think Jesus was pretty chuffed that the

friends had such strong faith, so he simply said, 'Son, your sins are forgiven.' Well, of course, that set some of the religious leaders off right away, accusing him of blasphemy and . . .

LINTON: (*Laughing*) Wo, I bet it did.

EVANS: He soon shut 'em up though. I tell you, I saw with my own eyes him smile at this paralysed man and say, 'Pick up your stretcher and go home. You're healed.' And this guy just got up, picked up his stretcher and pushed his way through the gobsmacked crowd. Amazing!

LINTON: Sounds pretty incredible.

EVANS: I promise you, it's the absolute truth.

LINTON: I believe you. I just wish I'd been here.

EVANS: Yeah. Look, I'm sorry about the roof, I feel awful. Do you think you'll be able to claim on your insurance all right?

LINTON: Yeah, don't worry about it. I'll just put on the claim form that it was an act of God! (*Laughs*) An act of God – get it? (*They both laugh as lights fade*)

TEACHING POINT

Jesus' miraculous power can deal with our physical and spiritual needs.

BIBLE REFERENCE

Mark 2:1–12

Frying Tonight

INTRODUCTION

This is a short piece to illustrate the miraculous catch of fish. We can assume from the Gospels that, at the time of this miracle, Simon would have been aware of Jesus' ministry (otherwise he probably would have totally ignored him). But to add the element of humour, he should be played focusing on his bad mood due to his unsuccessful night's fishing, rather than being in any way awestruck by Jesus.

Characters: SIMON; JAMES; JESUS.

SIMON and JAMES are on their boat, about to check for the last time if the night's fishing has been successful.

SIMON: What a night!

JAMES: Not one of our best.

SIMON: Not one of our best! It was an utter disaster, mate, an utter disaster! We've been here over ten hours, (*Emphatic*) ten hours. I've been through three thermoses full of my mum's coffee, and that's punishment enough in itself. I'm wearing two layers of Marks and Spencer's thermal undies, and I've still nearly frozen my derrière off, and what's it all been for? A big zero!

JAMES: Come on, are we gonna draw these nets in or not?

SIMON: I don't know if I can bear to. I tell you, if there's nothing in them, I'm gonna jump in and commit hara-kiri.

JAMES: Cheer up, Simon. Things could be worse.

SIMON: How?

JAMES: Well, er, now you mention it, they couldn't be much worse. Maybe you should just jump straight in.

SIMON: Oh, thank you. Come on then, let's get it over and done with. (*Action of drawing in the nets. This is followed by a pause and a despondent look down at the empty nets*)

SIMON: Look at that. Not a sausage.

JAMES: We weren't trying to catch sausages.

SIMON: (*Gives JAMES a dirty look*) Ha, ha! I wasn't asking for much, was I? Just a few cod. Maybe some haddock and pike. But look at that. Not even a minnow, sprat or tiddler.

JAMES: Hey, wait a minute. I think there's something caught in the net!

SIMON: (*Excited*) What? What is it?

JAMES: A tadpole.

SIMON: (*Deflated*) Oh, great! Give it a couple of months, and we can knock up a plate of frogs' legs.

JESUS: (*Enters and calls to SIMON and JAMES*) Ahoy there.

SIMON: Yeah, hello.

JESUS: Had a good night?

SIMON: Yeah! That is, if you think catching one tadpole and frostbite constitutes a good night.

JAMES: It's a bit of a sore point.

JESUS: Why don't you try where it's deeper?

SIMON: (*To JAMES*) Oh this is just what we need, a right know-it-all. (*Puts on a silly voice*) You don't wanna do it like that, you wanna do it like this. (*To JESUS*) Fisherman by trade, are you?

JESUS: No, carpenter.

SIMON: (*Laughing*) Did you hear that, James? A carpenter. (*To JESUS*) Know everything there is to know about the sea then, do you?

JESUS: Well, yes I do actually.

JAMES: (*Aside to SIMON*) I think we should give it a try. I've heard a lot about this guy and he knows what he's talking about.

SIMON: All right, all right! We've been working all night casting our nets into just about every nook and cranny, but if you say so, we'll try again. (*Choreographed movement downstage, then action of casting nets*)

SIMON/JAMES: (*Together*) 1-2-3-4-5-6-7-8-9-10. Draw! (*Action of drawing in nets. Pause. SIMON and JAMES look at nets amazed*)

SIMON: I don't Adam and Eve it!

JAMES: It's amazing!

JESUS: Mmm, quite a catch you've got there, fellas!

SIMON: (*Falls to knees*) Thank you so much, sir, but I think you should go now. You shouldn't be around filthy old sinners like me.

JESUS: Ah, not so fast, Simon. I've got a new job for you, still in the fishing line you'll be pleased to hear. Are you interested?

SIMON: Are you kidding? You try and stop me! (*He hugs JESUS and JAMES, then addresses the audience*) Ladies and gentlemen, contrary to earlier information, for the last time Simon and James' Fish and Chip Emporium will definitely be frying tonight! (*Fade to blackout*)

TEACHING POINT

In our everyday lives, we should expect to be amazed by Jesus' miracles.

BIBLE REFERENCE

Luke 5:1–11

Feeding the Five Million

INTRODUCTION

A common gripe people have about God is his apparent willingness to watch millions of people die of starvation in the Third World without intervening. Drawing on the teaching of the miracle of the feeding of the five thousand, this sketch shifts the onus onto us to make a difference in the world.

Characters: ONE, moody and cynical; TWO, a Christian. They can be played by males or females.

ONE and TWO enter. ONE is eating a Mars bar.

ONE: What a complete load of tripe.

TWO: What's up with you?

ONE: He must think we're all completely doo-lally!

TWO: (*Confused*) Who? What are you talking about?

ONE: That vicar! Drivelling on about Jesus feeding five thousand people.

TWO: Well, what's wrong with that?

ONE: Come on, didn't you hear him? (*Adopting old-fashioned vicar voice*) So Jesus did taketh the little boyeth's five loaveths and two fisheths, and verily he did waveth his magic wandeth, and lo and behold, there was enough for five thousand greedy piggeths to stuffeth their faces fulleth. (*Reverts to normal voice*) What a complete pile of poopeth! I mean, call me foolish, but under ordinary circumstances it just doesn't happen, does it? (*Takes a bite of his Mars bar*)

TWO: Well no, I'll give you that. Under ordinary circumstances, it doesn't. But this was a miracle, of course, and a miracle by its very nature has to be *extra*ordinary. If the story was about Jesus sharing a seventeen-pound turkey between a dozen people, it wouldn't exactly be a miracle, would it?

ONE: Well no, I suppose I see what you mean.

TWO: So what's the problem then?

ONE: Well I'll tell you what the crux of the problem is. It's all very well hearing stories two thousand years old about Jesus feeding five thousand people just 'cos they couldn't be bothered to go home for their tea, but here we are in the millennium era, a supposedly advanced society, and half the world's dying of starvation. If Jesus is so loving and wonderful, why can't he feed *them*?

TWO: Fair point. World starvation is a major problem. But if you think back to the story, Jesus didn't magically make the food appear from nowhere, did he? No, he used what was offered by the boy.

ONE: What? A piffling little bit of bread and fish?

TWO: It wasn't piffling at all. That lad gave Jesus all he had. You imagine if the world adopted the same attitude. God has provided enough food on this earth to feed us all until we're completely stuffed, with loads to spare. The problem isn't that God doesn't care or provide, it's that we're too greedy to share.

ONE: (*Guiltily puts his Mars bar away*) Well, I s'pose so.

TWO: Can you imagine the impact if individuals, governments and nations captured the real message of this simple story? It would be more than a piffling five thousand that would be fed – it'd be countless millions! Would you call that an ordinary circumstance?

ONE: No mate, I'd call it a flipping miracle!

TEACHING POINT

When we make sacrifices, Jesus can perform miracles.

BIBLE REFERENCE

Luke 6:1–15

Destination Tel Aviv

INTRODUCTION

In this sketch, the miracle of Jesus calming the storm is transferred from a boat on the Sea of Galilee to an aeroplane travelling from London to Tel Aviv. When rehearsing the sketch, it is important to define the area of the aeroplane, remembering the cramped surroundings. Some creative rehearsal will also be required to put together the vocal and physical effects of the aeroplane taking off and losing altitude.

Characters: NARRATOR; CANDY, the stewardess; SIMON; JAMES; JESUS.

Lights go up on SIMON, JAMES and JESUS seated in an aeroplane. JESUS is fast asleep. CANDY is standing at the rear of the plane with her back to the audience. They are all in frozen positions.

NARRATOR: Destination Tel Aviv. Jesus' world tour was proving a huge success. Following his sermon to a packed Wembley Stadium, he was flying directly back to Israel, accompanied by Simon and James, for what promised to be a homecoming extravaganza. (*NARRATOR becomes the voice of the pilot. 'Radio interference' noise at start and finish of all pilot's speeches*) Kkcchh. Good evening, ladies and gentlemen, and welcome to Cowboy Airlines flight CA624, travelling direct from London Heathrow to Tel Aviv. We have a journey-time tonight of around five and a half hours. Your stewardess this evening is Candy. I'll speak to you all again when we're approaching Tel Aviv. Thank you. Kkcchh. (*Freeze is broken, CANDY is preparing drinks. SIMON and JAMES start to talk*)

SIMON: He looks absolutely zonked.

JAMES: I'm not surprised. He hasn't had a day off in months.

SIMON: Still, he's looking forward to the homecoming.

JAMES: Yeah, it'll be good for him. Maybe we can find somewhere he can have a couple of days' peace and quiet.

SIMON: You're kidding, aren't you? I think he's proved that no place exists that can't be probed by the paparazzi!

JAMES: Fair point.

CANDY: Bum! Oh, sorry, but that's another one of my nails gone for a burton.

JAMES: (*Joking*) Don't worry. Our boss can heal that when he wakes up. (*SIMON gives him a nudge*)

CANDY: Ooh, is he a manicurist then?

SIMON: Well, he has been described as being all things to all men.

CANDY: That sounds a bit dodgy if you ask me.

NARRATOR: (*As captain*) Kkcchh. Cabin crew to give safety instructions and prepare for take-off. Kkcchh.

CANDY: Ooh, that's me. Right, ladies and gentlemen, I won't go into too many details 'cos it's a bit boring, but in the squillion-to-one chance we have a crash, there's a blow-up floaty thing under your seats. Put it on and pull the cord and jump out one of the exits here and here sharpish. You'll notice a little whistle hanging off your blow-up floaty thing, but to be honest with you, they're not a whole lot of use if you're floating around the middle of the Mediterranean Sea! Still, if there's a few of us, I suppose we could make up a group and do a version of the *Titanic* theme. Ha, ha just my little joke. Anyway, before we take off, I am pleased to inform you that tonight's in-flight movie is the drama *Alive*, about a group of rugby players whose jet crashes into the Andes, and they are all forced to eat each other to stay alive. Not amazingly suitable, I must admit, but they were a bit spartan for choice at Blockbusters. Please, put your seats in an upright position and fasten your seat belts, as the aircraft is about to take off. Thank you.

(*CANDY sits down. SIMON, JAMES and CANDY act out the take-off using actions and vocals. Lean back for take-off, pulling faces back to show gravity, then lean forward pushing faces back out, to show the plane levelling off*)

NARRATOR: (*As pilot*) Kkcchh. The seat-belt sign is now off, ladies and gentlemen, and I wish you all a pleasant journey. Kkcchh.

SIMON: I reckon I'll give the movie a miss. What do you think?

JAMES: Yeah, me too. Fancy a game of cards?

SIMON:	Nice one, yeah! (*Nudges JESUS who does not move*) He's well away. Just the two of us then. Pontoon?
JAMES:	OK. (*Starts dealing*)
CANDY:	Drinks?
SIMON:	Oh, yes please.
CANDY:	What about your mate, the manicurist?
SIMON:	No, I should leave him, he's very tired.
CANDY:	Not being funny, but I think I recognise him from somewhere.
JAMES:	Well, he has been in the headlines rather a lot recently. The Sermon at Wembley?
CANDY:	(*Catches on*) Oh, it's not . . . it is . . . it's that Jesus, innit? Oh you wait till I tell my mum. She thinks he's absolutely brilliant. 'Ere, I don't suppose he can tell me the secret of that trick of turning water into wine?
JAMES:	Well, not really, you see . . .
CANDY:	(*Interrupts*) No, I suppose he's in that magic circle thingy.
JAMES:	No, you don't understand. It's not a magic trick as such. There's a bit more to it than that.
CANDY:	Has he written any 'How to' books or anything?
SIMON:	No, he hasn't written any books at all. But a friend ours, Luke, is writing one just now.
CANDY:	Ooh, really? What's it called?
SIMON:	Um . . . *Luke*, I think.
CANDY:	*Luke*? Your mate Luke's writing a book about your mate Jesus, and the best title he can think of is *Luke*! Not very original, is it? Hardly likely to be a bestseller. He should think of a more catchy title like . . . *The Magical Manicurist*.

SIMON: (*Rolling his eyes*) Well, I'll suggest it to him. (*They all freeze*)

NARRATOR: At this moment, the storms outside struck one of the plane's engines, and the pilot was beginning to lose control. (*As worried captain*) Kkcchh. Please return to your seats, ladies and gentlemen, and fasten your seat belts. We're hitting some quite serious turbulence. Please stay seated and prepare for emergency positions. Our highly trained Cowboy Airlines stewardesses are well versed in remaining calm in emergency situations. Kkcchh. (*Cast break freeze*)

CANDY: Aaggghhhh! We're all gonna die! (*Short choreographed piece using actions and vocals showing loss of altitude*)

JAMES: Quick, see if you can wake him up.

SIMON: Jesus. (*More urgently*) Jesus! He's fast asleep.

CANDY: Asleep! How can he be asleep? Wake up, (*Hysterical*) wake up! (*Calmly adopts stewardess mode*) Ladies and gentlemen, we are currently plummeting to earth at 300 miles per hour. Assume the emergency positions by placing your head between your legs. Thank you for travelling Cowboy Airlines. (*SIMON and JAMES give up trying to wake JESUS and put their heads between their legs. CANDY sits on the floor in front of them with her head between her legs. We hear the sound effects of the diving plane. JESUS opens his eyes, calmly raises his arms and gives one loud clap. The effect of this is a moment's silence, then the comforting hum of the plane's engines resumes*)

SIMON:	(*Slowly gets up*) You're awake.
JESUS:	Of course. Just a little catnap. Are you all right?
SIMON:	Yeah. It's just, well, there was a terrible storm, and we were trying to wake you. To be honest, we got a little panicky.
JESUS:	Why do you always get so scared? Do you still not have any confidence in me? James, you can remove your head from between your legs now.
JAMES:	(*Sheepishly*) Thanks, boss.
JESUS:	And who is this on the floor? Can I help you up, young lady? (*JESUS helps CANDY up. She is rather disorientated*) Oh dear. It looks like you've broken one of your nails in all the kerfuffle.
CANDY:	(*Curtsies awkwardly, not knowing how to address JESUS*) Thank you, sir. I have . . . I think . . . I (*To JAMES*) Who is he? (*To JESUS*) Who are you exactly, if even storms do what you say?
JESUS:	I am who I am.
CANDY:	(*Confused*) Hey, that'll be a good title for your mate Luke's book – *I Am Who I Am*!
SIMON:	(*Smiles*) Yeah, I'll suggest it to him. (*All freeze and lights slowly fade to blackout*)

TEACHING POINT

Jesus is in total control, even of the elements.

BIBLE REFERENCES

Matthew 8:23–27; Mark 4:35–41; Luke 8:22–25

A Load of Codswallop

INTRODUCTION

In this sketch, two fishermen witness the miracle of Jesus walking on water. Roger takes what he sees at face value, whereas Arthur has a much more cynical outlook. The piece could be used to introduce the theme of belief versus cynicism.

For the best comedic effect, Arthur needs to be played rather over the top. Also, spend some time creating some funny costumes for the fishermen braving the stormy weather.

Characters: ARTHUR; ROGER.

Lights come up on ARTHUR and ROGER sitting centre stage fishing and drinking, wearing layers of rain-proof clothes. There is a period of silence during which beer is swilled and fishing lines are adjusted, etc. Optional storm sound effects would be helpful.

ARTHUR: Chuck us another beer.

ROGER: You'll be lucky.

ARTHUR: What?

ROGER: All gone, mate!

ARTHUR: Great! As if it ain't bad enough being stuck out in the pouring rain, now I've got to do it without alcoholic assistance.

ROGER: Well, they did forecast rain and gales.

ARTHUR: Weather forecasts! A load of codswallop, mate!

ROGER: They got it right tonight, didn't they?

ARTHUR: Well, it's the law of averages, innit? They've gotta be right sometimes. In my opinion, they don't get it right often enough to call it a forecast. It oughta be called the weather stab in the dark!

ROGER: (*Looking through binoculars*) They obviously didn't hear the forecast either.

ARTHUR: Who?

ROGER: Group of blokes out at sea. They seem to be having a few problems.

ARTHUR: Serves 'em right. Who'd take a boat out on a naff night like this?

ROGER: (*Concerned*) They really are having problems. Maybe we should call someone. Have a look. (*Offers ARTHUR binoculars*)

ARTHUR: Nah! I don't wanna have a look. They'll be all right. Give it a few minutes. It'll probably all calm down.

ROGER: (*Looks through binoculars again and screams*) Aagghhh! It's a ghost!

ARTHUR: What?

ROGER: There's a ghost out there. Have a look.

ARTHUR: Ghosts! A load of codswallop, mate.

ROGER: I'm not messing about, Arthur. See for yourself.

ARTHUR: No! I'm not looking. I know it ain't a ghost, and the reason I know it ain't a ghost, is 'cos they don't flippin' exist. It's probably some bloke dressed up in a load of white sheets.

ROGER: (*Looking through binoculars*) Oh, I think you could be right. Yeah, it is a man wearing white.

ARTHUR: There you are. What did I say?

ROGER: Slight problem though . . .

ARTHUR: What now?

ROGER: The bloke wearing white is walking on water.

ARTHUR: Walking on water? A load of codswallop, mate!

ROGER: He is! He's walking on water. Have a look.

ARTHUR: Nah! Anyway, if he is walking on water, it's probably 'cos he can't swim!

ROGER: You are such a cynic!

ARTHUR: That's what they call me, Arthur Cynical, and I'm proud of it.

ROGER: Don't you realise we could be witnessing a miracle?

ARTHUR: Miracles! A load of codsw–

ROGER: (*Interrupts*) Yes, I think I've got the message. In the world according to Arthur, everything's a load of codswallop.

ARTHUR: Well, you're so flippin' gullible. It drives me potty.

ROGER: I'm not gullible. But if something's blatantly obvious, I take it at face value.

ARTHUR: Mmmm. Come on then, have a look through your magic binoculars. What's happening now?

ROGER: (*Looks through binoculars*) What a nutter.

ARTHUR: What is it?

ROGER: One of the blokes is getting out the boat.

ARTHUR: Bit cold for a swim, innit?

ROGER: He's not going for a swim. He's walking on the water as well.

ARTHUR: Come off it! All these people walking around – are you sure they're not on an island?

ROGER: No, Mr Cynical, they're not on an island. Hang on a minute, he's starting to sink!

ARTHUR: Oh, at last, gravity triumphs.

ROGER: Wait . . . wait . . . wait . . . don't panic, it's all right. The one with the white cloak's got hold of him . . . he's got him back in the boat . . . it's all right, they're all back in the boat now. (*Offers ARTHUR binoculars*) Do you wanna have a look?

ARTHUR: Nah. Sounds like all the fun's over.

ROGER: Don't say I didn't offer.

ARTHUR: I won't.

ROGER: Well, that's another miracle.

ARTHUR: What now?

ROGER: The weather. All of a sudden the wind's died down and the rain's stopped.

ARTHUR: Oh yeah, so it has. It's turning out quite nice. I told you them weather forecasts were a load of codswallop! (*ARTHUR laughs, ROGER sighs. Lights fade to blackout*)

TEACHING POINT

In the face of miracles, are we cynics or believers?

BIBLE REFERENCE

Matthew 14:22–33

Bric-à-Brac Jack

INTRODUCTION

This piece is set following Jesus' raising of Lazarus from the dead. Jack, a sly antiques dealer, is hoping to get his hands on Lazarus' possessions; Mary, Lazarus' sister, is unsuccessfully trying to tell him that her brother is still alive. Lazarus' inevitable arrival throws Jack into bewildered confusion.

The piece does require prior knowledge of the Lazarus story, so is most suited to a church audience.

Characters: JACK; MARY; LAZARUS.

JACK: (*Smarmy*) Good afternoon, madam. I've come to offer my deepest condolences on the recent passing of your dearly beloved husband.

MARY: Oh. You mean Lazarus?

JACK: Yes.

MARY: He's my brother, actually.

JACK: I do beg your pardon. Still, the sibling bonds can be very close, wouldn't you agree, madam?

MARY: Absolutely.

JACK: Allow me to introduce myself. The name is Jack Trustworthy, owner of the antiques emporium on the high street. (*Hands MARY a business card*)

MARY: Well, it's very kind of you to come round, Mr Trustworthy, but it's really not necessary. You see . . .

JACK: (*Interrupts*) Of course it's necessary! It is my belief that when someone suffers the trauma of bereavement, those around them should stop at nothing to help in any way they can. Can I come in?

MARY: Er . . . I suppose so, but there really is something I should explain.

JACK: You need explain nothing to me, dear lady. I'm well versed in the grieving process and I'm sure I know exactly how you feel.

MARY: (*Aside*) I think that's highly unlikely!

JACK: At times like this, we just need to meditate and allow the . . . (*Breaks off suddenly as he spots a valuable chair*) Hel-lo!

MARY: What is it?

JACK: Have you had this chair long?

MARY: I think it's been in the family for a few generations.

JACK: (*Examines chair*) Yes, very nice. About 300 BC I would estimate.

MARY: Ooh, that old.

JACK: Mm, I wouldn't be surprised. (*Spots a table and drawers*) And this is quite remarkable too. Looks like a very early example of MFI.

MARY: How can you tell that?

JACK: Well, the leg's a bit wobbly and one of the drawers doesn't shut properly. Still, a lovely piece all the same.

MARY: Look, Mr Trustworthy . . .

JACK: (*Interrupts*) Call me Jack.

MARY: Thank you . . . Jack. There really is something I need to tell you, which makes your visit here rather superfluous.

JACK: (*Annoyed*) Don't tell me that dodgy Barry's been round to make you an offer already?

MARY: (*Confused*) No, I've never heard of any dodgy
           Barry.

JACK: (*Not listening*) He's a vulture! No scruples.
           Fancy him coming around before me – I mean,
           while the body's still warm.

MARY: The body's more than warm!

JACK: What?

MARY: That's what I've been trying to tell you.
           Lazarus isn't dead.

JACK: (*Pause, then laughs*) Oh dear, oh dear. Well, if
           that's true, he'll be in *The Guinness Book of
           Records* for holding his breath! (*Calms down*)
           Oh I'm sorry, madam, excuse me for laughing,
           but I thought you just said Lazarus isn't dead.

MARY: I did. He isn't. He's still with us.

JACK: (*Pause and gets wrong end of the stick.
           Continues sympathetically*) Oh, I see what you
           mean. Well, of course he's still with us. In our
           memories and in our minds and hearts. We can
           be with him even closer in the spirit, just not in
           the flesh.

LAZARUS: (*Enters, casually*) Afternoon, sis.

MARY: Hi, Lazarus.

JACK: Hello, Lazarus. (*Continues as before*) Yes, as I
           was saying, our bodies are merely the earthly
           garments by which . . . (*Stops and does a
           double-take as he clicks*) Hang on a minute.
           Lazarus . . . what the . . . how the . . . you're
           supposed to be dead!

LAZARUS: Yeah, I know. Slight change of plan. Good,
           isn't it? (*To MARY*) What's Bric-à-Brac Jack
           doing here?

JACK: Would you mind not calling me that! I don't
           own a bric-à-brac shop, it's an antiques empor-
           ium.

LAZARUS: Oh, sorry! So why are you round here then? Not chatting up my sister, I hope?

JACK: (*Defensively*) No, I was not! I was just . . . well, I was just . . .

MARY: (*Interrupts*) He was just about to make me an offer for all your furniture.

JACK: And a very generous offer it would have been too. (*Man to man to LAZARUS*) I was just trying to protect your sister from all those vultures who swoop in so callously after a death.

LAZARUS: (*Tries to usher JACK out*) Well, thanks, Bric-à-Brac Jack, but it won't be necessary now.

JACK: (*Revolted*) Uggghhh! Lazarus, you smell absolutely putrid!

LAZARUS: Oh yes, sorry! The embalming fluid's not quite worn off yet.

JACK: Oh, how revolting. (*Pause; he prods LAZARUS to check he's real*) So you actually died and got embalmed as well then?

LAZARUS: Yep, the full works.

JACK: So, how come you're still . . . well, you know . . .

LAZARUS: Let's just say I've got friends in very high places. (*Ushers out a totally confused JACK*) Goodbye.

MARY: (*Laughs and hugs LAZARUS*) Oh, it's so good to have you back. You're my walking, talking miracle. Bric-à-Brac Jack was right about one thing, though.

LAZARUS: What was that?

MARY: You do pong something chronic! (*They both laugh. Fade to blackout*)

TEACHING POINT

Jesus has power over everything, even death.

BIBLE REFERENCE

John 11:37–44

(B) TEACHING

Sermon on Mount Wembley

INTRODUCTION

This narration with actions is suitable for children to perform, and gives lots of scope for their creativity in the various actions that have to be worked out. It can be used for a performance or as a learn-by-doing teaching exercise. The key thing is that all the actions and mimes need to be very short and sharp, often just a couple of seconds to pull a pose. This will give the piece energy and pace, whereas long mimes and actions will draw it out unbearably.

Characters: NARRATOR; GROUP OF ACTORS (ideally no more than six to eight, especially if performing).

NARRATOR is standing to the side of the stage, ACTORS are standing in various poses facing audience.

NARRATOR: Wembley Stadium was chock-a-block. Never in its history had an event attracted so many thousands of people.
There were more people than at the last England home match. (*ACTORS break into a football crowd action then re-freeze*)
A bigger crowd than attended the famous Three Tenors show. (*ACTORS break into an operatic action then re-freeze*)
And unbelievably, even more than were at

the Spice Girls' concert.* (*ACTORS break into a Spice Girls action* then re-freeze*)

Around the stadium, dozens of vendors were selling all kinds of food, drink and knick-knacks. (*ACTORS call out in the style of market traders, e.g. Coke, ices, popcorn, T-shirts, programmes, etc.*)

But the crowd weren't interested. They had only come for one thing. As they grew impatient, they started Mexican waves (*ACTORS mime a Mexican wave*), and began chanting for the man they'd all come to hear. (*ACTORS break into a chant: 'Jesus', clap-clap-clap, 'Jesus', clap-clap-clap*)

They weren't to be disappointed. After a short wait, Jesus appeared from the wings and moved to the microphone centre stage. The crowd froze (*re-freeze in strained positions*), their jaws dropped (*ACTORS' jaws drop*) and they pricked up their ears ready to hear him speak. (*ACTORS all pull their ears out*)

He spoke non-stop for two hours – which may seem like a long time – but the crowd were totally transfixed. (*ACTORS continue to hold frozen jaws and ears pose*) Here, in true BBC-style, are the edited highlights.

Jesus spoke about happiness. (*ACTORS adopt frozen wide smiles*)

He said that the kingdom of heaven belongs to the poor in spirit (*ACTORS look sad*) so will be happy. (*ACTORS return to frozen wide smiles*)

---

* Replace with more appropriate topical reference as necessary.

The hungry shall be full (*ACTORS mime hunger and fullness*), so will be happy (*ACTORS return to frozen wide smiles*)

Those who cry shall be full of laughter (*ACTORS mime crying and laughter*), so will be happy. (*ACTORS return to frozen wide smiles*)

Those who make peace will be called sons of God (*ACTORS mime peace*), so will be happy. (*ACTORS return to frozen wide smiles*)

Those who are rejected and hated for being his friends will be rewarded in heaven (*ACTORS mime rejection and hate*), so will be happy. (*ACTORS return to frozen wide smiles*)

All that Jesus taught turned upside-down what the world thought, so all the people were totally confused. (*ACTORS mime total confusion*)

He then told the people to be an example to others, shining like lights in the world. (*ACTORS look bright and help one another*)

They were not to murder. (*ACTORS mime murder*)

Or even get angry. (*ACTORS mime anger*)

He told them that if anyone struck their right cheek (*ACTORS all slap right cheeks*), they had to turn the left one to their attacker as well. (*ACTORS all slap left cheeks*)

He said they must love their enemies. (*ACTORS mime loving your enemy*)

Jesus taught the people not to worry. (*ACTORS mime worry*)

And to be generous to those in need. (*ACTORS mime generosity*)
He told them that people who behaved like this would be storing up treasure in heaven. (*ACTORS mime storing treasure*)
At the end of his talk, Jesus prayed with the crowd (*ACTORS mime praying*), then left the stage. The packed Wembley crowd roared their approval (*ACTORS give three cheers to Jesus*), then left the stadium amazed and encouraged. There were no reports of crowd trouble. (*ACTORS sing to tune of football song 'You're Not Singing Any More' which is the same tune as 'Bread of heaven' in 'Guide Me, O Thou Great Jehovah':*)

ACTORS: Now we're smiling and we're laughing
'Cos we've got God on our side,
(he's on our side,)
'Cos we've got God on our side.
(*All exit. Blackout*)

TEACHING POINT

Jesus' teaching turns the world's perspective upside-down.

BIBLE REFERENCE

Matthew chapters 5–7

Clever Trevor and Thick Nick

INTRODUCTION

This piece is ideal to use with children, and has been written with very few stage directions, so that your group can create their own interpretation. Whether you use it as a rap, army-style chant or as a more basic rhyme, the key element the piece requires is a strong sense of rhythm. This can be built in rehearsal using clapping or, if preferred, a drum or basic percussion instrument. However you use it, the basic shape comprises one narrator performing the main story, with the chorus joining in for the responses. Appropriate actions should also be used.

The rhyme/chant is based on Jesus' teaching about those who build on rock and sand, found in Matthew chapter 7.

Characters: NARRATOR; CHORUS (any number).

NARRATOR:	There was once two boys called Trevor and Nick.
CHORUS:	Nice names.
NARRATOR:	Now Trevor was clever, but Nick was quite thick.
CHORUS:	What a shame.
NARRATOR:	They both were trying to woo a spouse.
CHORUS:	How sweet.
NARRATOR:	So they left their mums to build a house.
CHORUS:	That's neat.
NARRATOR:	They bowled on down to *Do It All*.
CHORUS:	Why's that?

NARRATOR: To buy bricks and mortar for building their walls.

CHORUS: Plus VAT.

NARRATOR: They chose a pretty spot to start their work.

CHORUS: Nice place.

NARRATOR: They made such a noise, the neighbours went berserk.

CHORUS: Shut yer face!

NARRATOR: They used their hammers and chisels, and saws and drillers, all morning and noon and night,
Then they built and they built and they built and they built and they built for the following fortnight.
Clever Trevor didn't race against the clock.

CHORUS: Too bad.

NARRATOR: He built his foundations on solid rock.

CHORUS: Clever lad.

NARRATOR: Thick Nick built his house in a manic rush.

CHORUS: Quick, quick!

NARRATOR: For his foundations he used a pile of sand and slush.

CHORUS: How thick.

NARRATOR: When they finished they both were over the moon.

CHORUS: We're chuffed.

NARRATOR: But the weatherman forecast storms very soon.

CHORUS: They're stuffed!

NARRATOR: Then the skies went dark, and we all got the nark, 'cos the weather was looking quite gloomy,
And it rained and it rained and it rained and it rained and it rained till the following Tuesday.

	Clever Trevor was looking very proud.
CHORUS:	So he should.
NARRATOR:	His house had weathered the storm, and stood its ground.
CHORUS:	How good.
NARRATOR:	Thick Nick didn't look so tickled pink.
CHORUS:	Why not?
NARRATOR:	Thanks to the storm his house did sink.
CHORUS:	What a flop!
NARRATOR:	So what's the moral of this tale?
CHORUS:	We don't know.
NARRATOR:	Well, listen up and make sure you don't fail.
CHORUS:	We won't.
NARRATOR:	You need to build your life on the Lord Jesus Christ, 'cos he is the ultimate rock. Follow him and pray, read your Bible every day, and he'll help you weather life's knocks.
ALL:	We need to build our lives on the Lord Jesus Christ, 'cos he is the ultimate rock. Follow him and pray, read our Bibles every day, and he'll help us weather life's knocks. Yes, he'll help us weather life's knocks, Yes, he'll help us weather life's knocks. (*Fade out repeating last line as ALL exit*)

TEACHING POINT

A firm foundation on Jesus is the only secure basis for life.

BIBLE REFERENCE

Matthew 7:21–29

Old Mac Jethro

INTRODUCTION

This piece is ideal either to perform with kids, or simply to use as a teaching aid for the message of this key parable. The narrator can either be an adult, or strong reader from the children, and any number of children can make up the acting ensemble. One child needs to be identified as Old Mac Jethro for the duration of the sketch.

If using the piece for performance, rehearsal will be needed for singing the new words to the tune of 'Old Macdonald Had a Farm'. Also make sure that the actions, which are repeated, are strong ones the children will remember.

Characters: NARRATOR; ACTORS (any number).

ACTORS stand in group across stage, not in a straight line. NARRATOR stands at side of stage.

NARRATOR: During his life on earth, Jesus told the crowds many stories to explain what God's kingdom would be like. One of the these stories was about a farmer called Old Mac Jethro. (*One ACTOR steps forward and makes a 'typical' farmer sound, e.g. 'Oo-arr, oo-arr'*) Now one day, Old Mac Jethro (*farmer noise*) went out to his fields to sow his corn seeds.

ACTORS: (*Singing to the tune of 'Old Macdonald Had a Farm', and acting out scattering*)

Old Mac Jethro had a farm, e–i–e–i–o.
And on that farm he scattered some seeds,
e–i–e–i–o.
With a scatter-scatter here, and a scatter-scatter there,
Here a scatter, there a scatter, everywhere a scatter-scatter.
Old Mac Jethro had a farm, e–i–e–i–o.
(*ACTORS freeze*)

NARRATOR: As the seeds were being sown by Old Mac Jethro (*farmer noise*), some fell on the path.

ACTORS: (*Singing and acting out pecking birds*)
Now some of those seeds landed on the path, e–i–e–i–o.
So the birds came along and pecked them all up, e–i–e–i–o.
With a peck-peck here, and a peck-peck there,
Here a peck, there a peck, everywhere a peck-peck.
Old Mac Jethro had a farm, e–i–e–i–o.
(*ACTORS freeze*)

NARRATOR: Some other seeds landed on rocky, stony soil.

ACTORS: (*Singing and acting out withering*)
Now some of that seed fell on rocky soil, e–i–e–i–o.
It grew a little bit, then the sun withered it, e–i–e–i–o.
With a wither-wither here, and a wither-wither there,
Here a wither, there a wither, everywhere a wither-wither.
Old Mac Jethro had a farm, e–i–e–i–o.
(*ACTORS freeze*)

NARRATOR: As Old Mac Jethro (*farmer noise*) continued to scatter the seeds, another batch were caught up in weeds and thorns.

ACTORS: (*Singing and acting strangulation*)
Some more of those seeds got caught in weeds and thorns, e–i–e–i–o.
And the seeds got killed by the strangling weeds, e–i–e–i–o.
With a eeurrch (*strangling noise*) here, and a eeurrch there,
Here a eeurrch, there a eeurrch, everywhere a eeurrch-eeurrch.
Old Mac Jethro had a farm, e–i–e–i–o.
(*ACTORS freeze*)

NARRATOR: But some of the seeds fell on good, healthy soil, and much to Old Mac Jethro's delight, (*farmer noise*) they grew into corn.

ACTORS: (*Singing and acting corn plants zooming up*)
Now the rest of those seeds fell on healthy soil, e–i–e–i–o.
They zoomed up quick to Old Mac Jethro's joy, e–i–e–i–o.
With a zoom-zoom here, and a zoom-zoom there,
Here a zoom, there a zoom, everywhere a zoom-zoom.
Old Mac Jethro had a farm, e–i–e–i–o.
(*ACTORS freeze*)

NARRATOR: The crowds had all enjoyed the story about Old Mac Jethro (*farmer noise*), but they hadn't understood its deeper meaning, so they all looked rather puzzled. (*ACTORS all look puzzled*)
So Jesus explained the story to them. In the story of Old Mac Jethro (*farmer noise*), the

seeds (*ACTORS do a quick scatter-scatter*) represent God's message and the soil represents the hearts of people who hear it.

Some people are like the path. Before they even have a chance to understand the message properly, the devil comes like a bird and snatches it away. (*ACTORS do a quick peck-peck*)

Others are like the rocky soil. They listen to the message happily, but as soon as they go through times of trouble, their interest withers away. (*ACTORS do a quick wither-wither*)

Still others are like the weeds and thorns. They hear and understand the message, but their care for money and what others may think chokes the message. (*ACTORS do a quick 'eeurrch'*)

But the healthy soil represents those who listen and understand the message, then put it into practice by the way they live their lives. So the good news grows and grows. (*ACTORS do a quick zoom*) So do you all think you understand the story now?

ACTORS: (*Together*) Yes!

NARRATOR: Are you sure?

ACTORS: (*Together*) Yes!

NARRATOR: Well, come on then. You'd better prove it.

ACTORS: (*Singing a rousing finale at speed*)
Ohhhhhh! With a zoom-zoom here and a zoom-zoom there,
Here a zoom, there a zoom, everywhere a zoom-zoom,
Eeurrch here, and a eeurrch there,

Here a eeurrch, there a eeurrch, everywhere a eeurrch-eeurrch,

Wither-wither here, and a wither-wither there,

Here a wither, there a wither, everywhere a wither-wither,

Peck-peck here, and a peck-peck there.

Here a peck, there a peck, everywhere a peck-peck,

Scatter-scatter here, and a scatter-scatter there,

Here a scatter, there a scatter, everywhere a scatter-scatter.

Old Mac Jethro had a farm (*Slow for big finish*), e–i–e–i–oooo! (*Blackout*)

TEACHING POINT

When you examine your life, which kind of soil best describes you?

BIBLE REFERENCE

Matthew 13:1–23

Do the Same

INTRODUCTION

This humorous reworking of the Good Samaritan parable is suitable for an all-age audience. To get the full benefit of it, a fair amount of rehearsal is necessary, but will be worth it to get the timing spot on. A big slice of dramatic licence has been used towards the end of the piece, allowing a possible scenario of the Samaritan continuing to beat up the Jewish traveller.

Characters: NARRATOR 1; NARRATOR 2; JEW; SAMARITAN (also doubles as bandit, priest and teacher).

JEW and SAMARITAN stand centre stage with backs to audience. NARRATOR 1 and NARRATOR 2 address audience, one from each side of the stage.

NARRATOR 1: Many years ago.

NARRATOR 2: Many, many years ago.

NARRATOR 1: (*Irritated*) Many, many, many years ago.

NARRATOR 2: Many, many, many . . .

NARRATOR 1: (*Interrupts*) Yes, all right! I think we've got the point. Carry on.

NARRATOR 2: The Jews hated the Samaritans. (*JEW turns to SAMARITAN and growls*)

NARRATOR 1: And the Samaritans hated the Jews. (*SAMARITAN turns to JEW and growls. They then have a short choreographed karate fight with sound effects*)

89

NARRATOR 2: The reason for the mutual hatred was so ancient, nobody could actually remember why it had started in the first place.

NARRATOR 1: During this period of history, a Jew was travelling from his home in Jerusalem. (*NARRATOR 1 holds up a 'Jerusalem' signpost*)

NARRATOR 2: To his destination in Jericho. (*NARRATOR 2 holds up a 'Jericho' signpost*)

NARRATOR 1: Unfortunately he didn't reach his destination, as he was attacked by a terrifying group of bandits. (*SAMARITAN as bandit comes flying out with a different costume, shouting at top of his voice. He grabs JEW by the neck. They freeze*)

NARRATOR 2: Or in the case of this low-budget production, a terrifying bandit. (*Over-pronounces the 't'*)

NARRATOR 1: The poor Jew was stripped of his clothes (*JEW's shirt is torn off*),

NARRATOR 2: Had all his money stolen (*Wad of notes is produced*),

NARRATOR 1: And was generally given a good working over by the bandit. (*Stylised fight scene with knee in groin, punch in face, karate chop on the neck, etc. Freeze*)

NARRATOR 2: The bandit then ran away with the booty, leaving the Jew half-dead beside the road.

SAMARITAN: (*As bandit, chanting*) You're going home in a Jewish ambulance. (*He runs off*)

NARRATOR 1: Fortunately, soon after this, a Jewish priest walked by on his way to mid-morning prayers. (*Nothing happens, so repeats loudly*) Fortunately, soon after this
. . .

SAMARITAN: (*Interrupts from offstage, mid-costume change*) Yes, all right, wait a second!

NARRATOR 2: He was taking a little longer than expected, as on the way home he'd popped into the kosher supermarket for his shopping.

(*SAMARITAN enters as priest, hands together, singing prayers*)

NARRATOR 1: He spotted the man lying by the roadside (*Stops in his tracks and looks at man*),

NARRATOR 2: And totally ignored him.

SAMARITAN: (*As a priest, singing prayers*) I'm crossing to the other side of the ro-ad. (*Exits*)

NARRATOR 1: Soon after this, a Jewish teacher came by on his way to afternoon lessons.

SAMARITAN: (*Rushes on as teacher, new costume all askew and hanging out*) Repeat after me, children, the Ten Commandments in chronological order.

NARRATOR 2: He spotted the man lying in the street (*Stops in his tracks and looks at man. Looks around to see if he is being observed, then steps over man and walks off muttering the Ten Commandments*), and totally ignored him.

NARRATOR 1: Then, at last, through the haze of the shimmering sunshine, came the despised Samaritan. (*SAMARITAN enters*)

NARRATOR 2: And as he saw his enemy lying half-dead on the roadside, he grasped the opportunity to pummel his head in and finish his enemy off. (*SAMARITAN starts to kick JEW's head in*)

NARRATOR 1: Wait a minute, wait a minute! (*To SAMARITAN*) Will you stop it!

(*SAMARITAN freezes. NARRATOR 1 turns back to NARRATOR 2*) You daft pin-brain, that's not how the story ends!

NARRATOR 2: Innit?

NARRATOR 1: No!

NARRATOR 2: Well, it should do, if you ask me.

NARRATOR 1: Well, luckily I'm not asking you.

NARRATOR 2: Look, pal. There's a Jewish guy half-dead in the road, right?

NARRATOR 1: Right.

NARRATOR 2: Now, a Jewish priest can't be bothered to help, and neither can a Jewish teacher, right?

NARRATOR 1: Right.

NARRATOR 2: Well, if they can't be bothered to help, no one's gonna believe that a Samaritan, his worst enemy is gonna help, are they?

NARRATOR 1: Oh, you nincompoop. That's the whole point of the story.

SAMARITAN: (*Still holding freeze*) Will you two hurry up and decide?

NARRATOR 1/2: (*Together*) Shut up! (*SAMARITAN continues freeze*)

NARRATOR 1: The whole point of the story is how to truly love your neighbour.

NARRATOR 2: Oh!

NARRATOR 1: Anyone can love their family and friends, but to love your neighbour in the way that Jesus spoke about means showing kindness to everyone, including our enemies.

NARRATOR 2: Oh, that's beautiful, man. You'd better finish it off.

NARRATOR 1: OK. Unfreeze. (*SAMARITAN shows relief as he breaks freeze*) Rewind. (*SAMARITAN acts out a fast rewind of kicking JEW's head and walks backwards offstage. This needs to be carefully planned for best effect*) Then, at last, through the haze of the shimmering sunshine, came the despised Samaritan. (*SAMARITAN enters*) He knelt beside the man, poured TCP on his wounds (*JEW screams*) and then took him away to be nursed back to health. (*SAMARITAN puts JEW on his back and carries him offstage*) And that, my friend, is how you truly show love to your neighbour.

NARRATOR 2: Showing kindness to everyone, even those people you're not all that keen on.

NARRATOR 1: Precisely. (*To audience*) So, ladies and gentlemen, boys and girls, all you have to do now is – go and do the same. (*Pause as they stare into the audience*)

NARRATOR 2: Go on then! Go and do the same! (*Blackout*)

TEACHING POINT

'Loving our neighbour' includes helping anyone in need, not just our family and friends.

BIBLE REFERENCE

Luke 10:25–37

Ask, Seek, Knock

INTRODUCTION

This humorous piece illustrates the parable of the friend at midnight, found in Luke chapter 11. The sketch will work using just two people, or alternatively, if more are available, the short bursts of the song 'Seek ye first' can be provided using a small vocal ensemble. If this is an impossibility, the singing will need to be provided by the actor playing Frank.

Characters: FRANK, the friend at midnight; KEN, the homeowner; optional vocal ensemble.

VOCAL: (*Singing*) Ask and it shall be given unto you.

FRANK: (*Knocks on door*) Hello! Anybody home?

KEN: (*Groggy*) Who's there?

FRANK: Ah, hello. My name's Frank, I live a few doors down.

KEN: Have you any idea what the time is?

FRANK: The time? Yes, it's precisely twenty past midnight.

KEN: (*Fuming*) Twenty past midnight! What do you want at this unearthly hour?

FRANK: Well, it's a bit embarrassing really. Some friends of mine have dropped in, completely unexpected needless to say, and, well, to be totally frank with you, I've got less food in the cupboard than Old Mother Hubbard!

KEN: Well, thank you for being so frank, Frank, but frankly I don't think it's my problem.

FRANK: I know it's a pain, but if you could just see your way clear to bunging us a couple of loaves of Hovis, I'll be on my way.

KEN: Listen, mate, I've locked the doors for the night, all right? Now before you wake the whole house up, do me a favour and buzz off!

FRANK: Well, if that's your final word on the matter. . .

KEN: (*Emphatic*) Yes, it is!
(*Pause as FRANK considers his next move*)

VOCAL: (*Singing*) Seek and ye shall find.
(*FRANK knocks on door*)

KEN: What?

FRANK: Frank here again.

KEN: Oh, you do surprise me!

FRANK: It's about those couple of loaves of Hovis again. I know it's a real pain for you, but I really am quite desperate.

KEN: Are you totally deranged?

FRANK: Sorry.

KEN: Look! It's past midnight, and if you don't quit hammering on my door, I'm gonna come out there and rearrange your face.

FRANK: Oh, I don't mind. Any chance you can bring the bread out while you're at it?

KEN: Good grief! Are you brainless, man? My two kids are fast asleep in here. Any more of this racket and you'll wake the pair of them up.

FRANK: Oh, how sweet. You've got kids? What are their names?

KEN: Tom and Becky.

FRANK: Oh, what lovely names. How old are the little cherubs?

KEN: (*Proudly*) Well, Becky was just nine last month on the twelfth, and little Tommy is . . . (*Stops himself in realisation of situation, then becomes very annoyed*) It doesn't matter how old they are. I can't believe I'm discussing my kids with an escaped lunatic at half past twelve at night.

FRANK: (*Checks watch*) Twenty-five past, actually.

KEN: I don't care! Now for the last time, (*Shouts*) go away!

FRANK: (*Aside*) Oh dear, I don't think I'm very popular. (*Pause as once again FRANK considers his next move*)

VOCAL: (*Singing*) Knock and it shall be opened unto you. (*FRANK knocks on door*)

KEN: (*Screaming through gritted teeth*) In the name of all things holy, what do you want, Frank?

FRANK: (*Surprised*) Hey, how did you know it was me?

KEN: Just a wild stab in the dark. Now, what is it?

FRANK: I just wanted to check that little Tom and Becky are still all tucked up and asleep.

KEN: Yes, thanks. Still fast asleep, which is the only reason you're still breathing.

FRANK: Good. Well, as they're such heavy sleepers, do you think passing me that bread is really such an unreasonable request?

KEN: (*Defeated*) No, Frank. Knocking on my door after midnight to borrow bread is not unreasonable at all. In fact, I'm the unreasonable one for not trampling over my family straight away to fetch it. I can assure you I will severely reprimand myself in the very near future for my ungentlemanly behaviour. (*He goes to fetch bread*)

FRANK: Well, don't be too hard on yourself now. Some people would have been quite rude and unhelpful at such a request.

KEN: (*Returns with bread and finally opens door*) Two fresh loaves of Hovis.

FRANK: Oh, thank you so much. Are you sure it's no trouble?

KEN: None at all! It's been a pleasure. What are neighbours for?

FRANK: That's kind. If I can ever repay the favour . . .

KEN: Don't mention it. Now, if you don't mind, I'll get back to bed. I've got an early start in the morning.

FRANK: Oh please, go right ahead. (*KEN exits. FRANK turns to audience*) Ah, isn't that kind? Bread from heaven.

VOCAL: (*Singing stirring finale*) Hallelu, hallelujah. (*Blackout*)

TEACHING POINT

Jesus' lesson through this parable is that we should be persistent in our prayers.

BIBLE REFERENCE

Luke 11:5–10

The Prodigal

INTRODUCTION

This piece is a basic retelling of the Parable of the Prodigal Son rather than one that expounds its message. You can use it in a number of contexts: with children you can teach the story by letting them perform it; in a performance context, you can use the narrated style as written, or a slick group of four or five actors could share out the lines and work on the movements to create a really polished piece.

Whichever way you choose, the piece should be fast-moving with short actions followed by freezes, making it very stylised. The actor playing the prodigal son stays in character for the whole sketch; everyone else plays multiple parts.

Characters: NARRATOR; ensemble of *actors* (any number).

NARRATOR: There was once a man, who had two sons. (*Actors playing these parts step forward*) The older son enjoyed dutifully working for his father. (*Acts working with forced unnatural smile. Freeze*) But the younger son found his work totally boring. (*Acts boredom, e.g. picking his nose. Freeze*)

One day the younger son had a bright idea. (*Act out a bright idea. Freeze*) He asked his father for his share of the property there and then, while he was young enough to enjoy it.

(*Son grabs father and says something along the lines of, 'Give us me money!' Freeze*) He was shocked when his father immediately agreed. (*Father says 'OK' and hands him a pile of money. The son falls back in amazement and is caught by other actors. Freeze*) With his new-found wealth, he rushed out to buy a new car. (*Act out a car, while vocalising the Grand Prix theme tune. Freeze*) Wooed by the drop-dead gorgeous babe on the advert, he opted for a Renault Clio. (*Two actors call out, 'Papa, Nicole, Nicole, Papa'. Freeze*) He squandered his money on wild parties (*Sing and dance to a quick blast of a current popular song. Freeze*), loose women (*Female actors flirt around him asking for a dance/good time, etc. Freeze*), gambling (*Acts out shaking and rolling dice with vocal encouragement from other actors. Freeze*), and boozing. (*Acts picking up drink then downing it in one with more vocal encouragement from other actors. Freeze*) This resulted in many fights (*Actors perform short energetic stylised fight. Freeze*), and in him eventually running out of money. (*He turns pockets inside out and cries out, 'I'm skint!' Other actors turn their noses up. Freeze*) Coincidentally, at this time, all his so-called friends (*Actors all pull forced friendly smiles. Freeze*) decided to do a runner, leaving him all alone. (*Actors take three steps back then quickly turn around. Freeze*) At this time, there was also a famine, and the son began to starve. (*Acts hunger and sits *in corner, dozing. Freeze*) He would day-dream about the food he used to enjoy before he left home. (*Actors sing theme tunes from food adverts, e.g. 'I feel like Chicken Tonight', 'Only the crumbliest, flakiest chocolate'. Each time the son wakes up they stop. As he dozes off again, they start a different tune. Freeze*)

Finally, in desperation, he persuaded a local farmer to give him some work. (*One actor identifies himself as a farmer and starts singing, 'I am a cider drinker' in an exaggerated 'country' accent. Freeze*) He was put to his task of feeding the pigs. (*Actors all become pigs, snorting and oinking, etc. Son feeds them reluctantly. Freeze*) He was so hungry, he began to eat the same slops as he was feeding to the pigs. (*He joins pigs, jostling for food. Freeze*)

All of a sudden inspiration struck. (*Act out sudden flash of inspiration. Freeze*) His father's workers were treated better than he was. He could return to his father, apologise and offer himself as a servant. So he headed for home. (*He walks to one end of stage, his father to the opposite side. Freeze*)

When his father saw him, he threw his arms open and ran to greet his son. (*They both hold out arms and run in slow motion singing theme tune to* Chariots of Fire. *Freeze*) In his excitement, the father called for the finest robe to be brought for his son to wear (*One actor places robe on son. Freeze*), a diamond-studded ring for his finger (*Actor places ring on his finger. Freeze*) and a pair of Kickers for his feet. (*Actor places shoes on his feet*)

At this point, the fatted calf was looking extremely worried (*An actor becomes a worried-looking fatted calf. Freeze*), and rightly so, as the father called for him to be immediately slaughtered. (*Actors cheer and jump on calf, killing him violently. Freeze*)

Meanwhile, the older brother was sulking outside. (*Act out sulking*) He was complaining that it was his disobedient little brother who was getting the red-carpet treatment, whereas he'd been the good guy for years and got nothing. (*Act out stomping and call out, 'It's so unfair!' Freeze*) But his father put his arm around his son and explained . . . (*Actors start humming theme from Hovis advert. This peters out after NARRATOR gives them a dirty look*) As I was saying, his father explained that it was only right to celebrate his brother's return: they'd thought he was dead, but he'd come back to them alive; they'd thought he was lost, but he'd been wonderfully found!

So the scene was set for the biggest knees-up in living history. (*Act out celebration with all actors linked together doing the cancan or similar for the grand finale*)

TEACHING POINTS

1. When people turn to Christ, we should celebrate, regardless of their previous circumstances or lifestyle.

2. God will always welcome us, if we repent and ask his forgiveness.

BIBLE REFERENCE

Luke 15:11–32

Five Hundred Excuses

INTRODUCTION

This sketch is based on the Parable of the Great Feast in Luke chapter 14. 'Sir' is a very down-to-earth and friendly character and Charles is his somewhat sarcastic and typically English butler. It should be played for laughs and is suitable in any context although, in an evangelistic setting, there would need to be some form of talk.

Characters: SIR; CHARLES.

SIR: Ah, there you are, Charles. Is everything ready?

CHARLES: Yes, Sir, everything has been arranged according to your specification.

SIR: Good. So the guests will have something to eat and drink as soon as they arrive?

CHARLES: Yes, Sir. On arrival they'll be offered champagne cocktails and canapés.

SIR: Can o' peas? I don't wanna give my guests no cheap tinned rubbish.

CHARLES: No, Sir, not cans of peas, canapés.

SIR: Oh! What are they then?

CHARLES: Little segments of bread or pastry with various savoury toppings, Sir.

SIR: Well, whatever you say, Charles. You know best.

CHARLES: Precisely, Sir. (*Slight pause*) If I might have a quiet word with you, Sir, about a rather delicate issue.

SIR: In a minute, Charles, in a minute. I just want to
              check the catering arrangements with you first.

CHARLES: If Sir insists.

SIR: Now, for the main course, have you prepared
              the fatted calf?

CHARLES: Of course, Sir. We've slaughtered and roasted
              a whole herd.

SIR: And what about the starters? I don't want no
              naff prawn cocktails.

CHARLES: Heaven forbid that I should ever serve prawn
              cocktails, Sir. The chef has prepared medal-
              lions of salmon on a bed of dill and parsley.

SIR: Ooh, sounds scrummy. And, most impor-
              tantly, what's for afters?

CHARLES: (*Confused*) Afters, Sir?

SIR: You know, afters. Pudding, seconds . . . des-
              serts!

CHARLES: Ah, desserts. Yes, there will be a choice of
              charlotte russe, crème caramel and, of course,
              Sir's favourite, spotted dick and custard.

SIR: Mmm! That's what I like to hear.

CHARLES: Now Sir, if I could just speak to you on this
              quite pressing matter . . .

SIR: (*Irritated*) Oh, what is it, Charles? The guests
              will be arriving any minute now.

CHARLES: Well, it was about the guests I needed to speak
              with you, Sir.

SIR: What about them? Come on Charles, spit it
              out, man.

CHARLES: Well, Sir, it seems there may be a slight short-
              age in the guest department.

SIR: (*Confused*) A slight shortage? What are you
              talking about?

CHARLES: We've had a number of replies this morning
              expressing sincerest apologies for absence.

SIR: Well, I suppose when you invite five hundred people, it's inevitable a few won't turn up. Exactly how many aren't coming then?

CHARLES: Five hundred, Sir.

SIR: Five hundred? What? I've invited five hundred people to this flippin' banquet, and five hundred have turned me down?

CHARLES: I'm afraid so, Sir.

SIR: (*Calculating in his head*) So, five hundred minus . . . five hundred . . . Hang on! That means no one's coming!

CHARLES: Your powers of subtraction astound me, Sir.

SIR: Blimey O'Riley! So why aren't they coming then?

CHARLES: (*Picks up full dustbin liner, empties out hundreds of cards*) Take your pick, Sir!

SIR: (*Picks up a few cards and reads*) 'Thank you for your kind invitation, but unfortunately I can't attend as my pet hamster Henry is going to the vet's to have his prostate gland sorted' . . . 'Can't come tonight, it's my bath night' . . . 'Sorry I won't be there tonight, as things are rather hotting up between Ricky and Bianca in *EastEnders*'. Oh, for goodness' sake, this is absolutely pathetic.

CHARLES: Quite so, Sir, absolutely pathetic. It does also leave me in a slight predicament.

SIR: What's that then, Charles?

CHARLES: Well, what does Sir require me to do with five hundred salmon medallions, a herd of roasted fatted calves and half a ton of spotted dick?

SIR: (*Sighs and pauses to think*) I've got it! We'll have to invite some other people.

CHARLES: Invite who exactly, Sir?

SIR: (*Getting excited*) Anyone . . . everyone!

	For starters, what's your missus doing tonight?
CHARLES:	Clarissa? I think she was staying in to do some macramé, Sir.
SIR:	Invite her, and any of your family, friends and neighbours.
CHARLES:	Well, I must say, Sir, that's extremely generous of you.
SIR:	Not at all, Charles. If the people I invite are going to turn me down, I'll swing the doors wide open. I want you to go into the streets and invite anybody you see.
CHARLES:	(*Dismayed*) Anybody?
SIR:	Yeah, I don't mind who – rich, poor, young, old, homeless, beggars, anyone. And if when you've been all round, there's still room, we'll even invite some folk from . . . (*enter nearby area to you that is often ridiculed*)
CHARLES:	(*Repeats place-name in disgust*) Oh, really Sir, that would be the limit!
SIR:	Chop, chop, Charles! On your way. Round 'em all up.
CHARLES:	Whatever Sir says. (*CHARLES exits, mumbling to himself*)
SIR:	(*Pauses for thought, glancing around*) Right, I think I'll grab first choice of the canapés. (*SIR exits. Fade to blackout*)

TEACHING POINT

Jesus Christ's invitation is for everyone, but are you accepting or politely making your excuses?

BIBLE REFERENCE

Luke 14:15–24

You're Going Down!

INTRODUCTION

This piece is based on the Parable of the Unforgiving Servant. The actors are all on stage for the whole sketch. During the short musical interludes and when any character is not involved, they hold an appropriate freeze position. The piece should be fairly fast-moving and there should be no pregnant pauses in between the short scenes.

Characters: NARRATOR; ROBERT; BOSS; FREDDY.

As lights go up, all actors are on stage in an appropriate freeze position. There is a short loud blast of music which is played at either end of each scene.

NARRATOR: Scene One. The Boss summons Robert. (*Short loud blast of music*)

BOSS: Hello, Robert.

ROBERT: Hello, Boss.

BOSS: Keeping well?

ROBERT: Been better, Boss.

BOSS: Mmmm. (*Refers to little black book*) A million-pound loan for gambling debts at Dicey Derek's Casino.

ROBERT: Yes, Boss.

BOSS: Another loan of half a million for a small business venture, which has recently gone under, so I understand.

ROBERT: Yes, Boss.

BOSS: And on top of that, there's your interest

107

	payments, at a very generous rate of 22.4%, which as of today run to four hundred and thirty-seven thousand quid.
ROBERT:	(*Gulps*) A very generous rate, Boss.
BOSS:	Let's round it all up, for tidiness' sake. You owe me two million quid! Have you got it?
ROBERT:	(*Floundering*) Well, there's various things I've got going at the moment, ongoing concerns, revenue I'm expecting to come in any time, a few outstanding debts . . . No, I haven't.
BOSS:	(*Pause*) Oh dear!
ROBERT:	Oh dear?
BOSS:	Oh dear, oh dear, oh dear!
ROBERT:	So, what are you going to do to me?
BOSS:	(*Sighs*) Do you really want to know?
ROBERT:	No, not really.
BOSS:	Well, I'm gonna tell you anyway. Firstly I'll need to sell off all your assets, properties, possessions, etcetera, etcetera, then I'll declare you bankrupt. After that, I'll sling you into prison, and sell your wife and kids into slavery.
ROBERT:	(*Falls to knees*) Oh no, please, Boss!
BOSS:	Don't take it personally, Robert. It's only business.
ROBERT:	(*Grovelling*) I beg you, Boss, I entreat you! Show compassion, show mercy.
BOSS:	Oh please, stop grovelling. It doesn't become a grown man.
ROBERT:	(*Snivelling*) Please, Boss, just give me time. I swear I'll pay you back, every last penny.
BOSS:	(*Pauses to think while grovelling and snivelling continue*) Oh, what the 'eck! I tell you what, why don't I just forget the debt?

(*ROBERT continues to grovel and snivel incoherently*)

BOSS: All right, I've said I'd clear the debt. Just watch the snot down my Armani suit!

ROBERT: (*Further snivelling which stops suddenly when he clicks what BOSS has said*) What did you just say?

BOSS: I said watch your snot down my suit!

ROBERT: No, not that bit. Before, about the debt.

BOSS: Forget it. I'll write it off! I'm loaded anyway. But remember this favour I've done you, and maybe you can pass it on to someone else.

ROBERT: (*Ecstatic*) Yes, Boss! I will, Boss! Thanks, Boss! (*They freeze; short loud blast of music*)

NARRATOR: Scene Two. Robert bumps into Freddy Fingers. (*Short loud blast of music*)

ROBERT: Oi, Freddy Fingers!

FREDDY: (*Nervous*) Ah hello, Rob. How lovely to see you.

ROBERT: Shut up, Freddy! I think you know what I want.

FREDDY: I don't think so, Rob, no!

ROBERT: Well, I'll tell you what I want, what I really really want.

FREDDY: A zigger zig ah?

ROBERT: No! What I want is the money you owe me.

FREDDY: Oh that! Come on, Rob, it's only a measly five hundred quid. Can't you give me a bit more time?

ROBERT: I'm afraid not. You've always got your fingers in everyone's pie, and it's time you learnt a lesson. I want my money now, or I'm having you arrested!

FREDDY:	(*Falls to knees*) I beg you, Rob. I entreat you! Show compassion, show mercy.
ROBERT:	No, I'm sorry. As they say in the movies, Freddy, you're going down! (*They freeze; short loud blast of music*)

NARRATOR:	Scene Three. Freddy makes a phone call. (*Short loud blast of music*)
BOSS:	(*Speaking on phone*) Hello, who's that?
FREDDY:	Hello, Boss. It's Freddy. Freddy Fingers.
BOSS:	Hey, Freddy, it's been a long time. What are you up to nowadays?
FREDDY:	Well, at this precise moment I'm an honoured guest of Her Majesty's.
BOSS:	Oh dear, oh dear, oh dear! What scrapes have you been getting into now?
FREDDY:	Oh, you know, the usual. A bit of debt.
BOSS:	How much this time?
FREDDY:	Five hundred quid.
BOSS:	Five hundred! Is that all? Who's sent you down for a piffling five hundred quid?
FREDDY:	Well, that's where I was hoping you could help me, Boss. It's one of your respected employees. I thought you could maybe have a word and persuade him to give me a bit more time. I will pay it back, I give you my word.
BOSS:	I trust you, Freddy. Thousands wouldn't. Go on then, I'll have a word. Who is it?
FREDDY:	Cheers, Boss. It's Rob.
BOSS:	(*Stunned*) Robert!
FREDDY:	Yeah, Boss, Robert. He's still with you, isn't he?
BOSS:	Oh yes, Freddy. He's still with me. Don't worry about a thing. I'll sort it out for you.

FREDDY:	Cheers, Boss, you're a diamond.
BOSS:	(*Thinking*) You bet I'll sort it all out. (*They freeze; short loud blast of music*)

NARRATOR:	Scene Four. The Boss summons Robert, part two. (*Short loud blast of music*)
ROBERT:	What can I do for you, Boss?
BOSS:	You can tell me something I've heard isn't true.
ROBERT:	It isn't true!
BOSS:	I've had a phone call from Freddy Fingers.
ROBERT:	Ah!
BOSS:	Yes, ah indeed! He says he's doing a spell of porridge 'cos he can't pay you back a small debt. Surely this can't be true.
ROBERT:	No, it's not true. (*Pause*) Yes, Boss, it's true.
BOSS:	How could you? I wrote off your debt of two million pounds simply because you asked me, and you can't even find it in your heart to write off someone else's for five hundred. You've upset me, Robert, you've truly upset me.
ROBERT:	I'm sorry, Boss, I –
BOSS:	(*Cuts in*) Too late! I've only got one thing left to say to you, Robert. You're going down! (*Freeze and final short loud blast of music. Blackout*)

TEACHING POINT

In the same way Jesus forgives us, he expects us to forgive others.

BIBLE REFERENCE

Matthew 18:21–35

A Nice Slice of Talent

INTRODUCTION

In the church, there are so many giftings, the problem is some people don't realise or utilise the gifts they have, whereas others are convinced they have gifts they clearly haven't got! This sketch, based on the Parable of the Talents, takes a look at Jesus' teaching on giftings, and, most importantly, how we use what we've been given. Suitable for any age audience, the sketch needs to have plenty of ensemble rehearsal and be performed with lots of pace and energy.

Characters: NARRATOR; GUV; TOM; DICK; HARRY.

GUV, TOM, DICK and HARRY are in a semi-circle facing the audience. NARRATOR is at centre stage also facing audience. The five actors open the sketch with a vocal trumpet-style fanfare. NARRATOR steps forward.

NARRATOR: (*Proclaiming*) A Nice Slice of Talent! (*Cast applaud and 'bravo' as NARRATOR bows. After a couple of seconds, he stops bowing and suddenly holds up his hand in readiness to begin the story. As he does this, the others stop cheering immediately*) Long ago and far away, there was a man who owned his very own building business.

GUV: I own my very own building business.

NARRATOR: His name was Guv.

112

GUV:	My name is Guv. (*NARRATOR and GUV change places*)
NARRATOR:	Now Guv had three loyal employees whose names were . . .
GUV:	(*Sergeant major style*) Tom!
TOM:	(*Salutes*) Guv'nor!
GUV:	(*Sergeant major style*) Dick!
DICK:	(*Salutes*) Guv'nor!
GUV:	(*Sergeant major style*) And 'arry!
HARRY:	(*Salutes*) Guv'nor!
NARRATOR:	Now Guv hadn't had a holiday for years, so thought it was time he took a trip.
GUV:	Methinks it's time I took a trip.
NARRATOR:	He decided he would travel the world by plane, train and automobile (*GUV mimes each of these. TOM, DICK and HARRY can help provide suitable sound effects*), and leave in charge his three loyal employees . . .
TOM:	Tom,
DICK:	Dick,
HARRY:	And 'arry.
NARRATOR:	But before he left, being a man of humungous generosity, he decided to give each of his boys a gift.
GUV:	Tom, you've always been a good loyal worker, and as a special gift to you, I would like to give you a guitar and five thousand pounds.
TOM:	Cheers, Guv, that's absolutely brill.
NARRATOR:	Tom was really chuffed and began planning in his mind how best he could use Guv's generous gift. Next to be called was Dick.
GUV:	For you, Dick, I have *The Complete Works of William Shakespeare* and two thousand

	pounds. I'm looking forward to seeing how you can use it.
DICK:	Thanks, Guv. I'll do my best to make a good return on your generous investment.
NARRATOR:	Dick was also pleased, and pondered how he could best use Guv'nor's gift. Last, but certainly not least, was Harry.
GUV:	For you, Harry, I have a top-of-the-range pair of running shoes and a thousand pounds.
HARRY:	Thanks, Guv. (*He turns his nose up at his gift*)
NARRATOR:	Harry was not pleased. He began to mumble (*HARRY mumbles*) and groan. (*HARRY groans*) He was totally unhappy with what Guv had trusted him with.
HARRY:	Wow! A pair of trainers and a measly thousand. Why couldn't I have had the guitar, or at least a couple of grand? It's not fair!
NARRATOR:	So, having got his affairs in order, Guv prepared to go on his trip of a lifetime. Over the course of a year, he packed in a lifetime of experiences. (*During this section, TOM, DICK and HARRY join in with GUV to break into poses and short mimes illustrating his holiday*) He danced through Scotland. (*TOM, DICK and HARRY vocalise bagpipes as GUV does a Scottish dance*) Partied across Buenos Aires. (*Act out a quick burst of the conga*) Hitched his way across America. (*All thumb a lift with other hand on heart humming a burst of the American anthem*) Sung his way across France. (*GUV breaks*

into a mini version of 'Chanson d'amour'; the others fill in the appropriate rat-a-tat-a-tats) Yodelled his way through the Swiss Alps. (*All break into a yodel*) Ballet danced through the Bolshoi. (*Whistle theme from* The Nutcracker *with appropriate ballet movements*) And naturally got his head kicked in at an England football game. (*Short choreographed fight and short extract from 'Football's coming home'*) All in all though, he felt it had been a worthwhile trip.

GUV: Methinks it's been a truly worthwhile trip.

NARRATOR: During his trip, Tom, Dick and Harry had been using their gifts in a variety of ways and Guv was looking forward to seeing the fruit of their labours. First of all on his return, he called Tom to give an account.

TOM: Guv, I used the five thousand to get training in rock guitar and putting a band together. We've got a record deal and our debut album has gone platinum. (*TOM launches into a solo performance. This can either be performed by the actor or by using a backing tape which is mimed along to. However it is done, it should be short and energetic, involving a lot of Jimi Hendrix style guitar antics*)

GUV: (*Rubs his ear*) Well done, good and faithful employee.

NARRATOR: Next to give his account was Dick.

DICK: Well, Guv, I used the two thousand to get professional training in Shakespearean acting and iambic pentameter, and I'm going to be playing Hamlet at the RSC next season. (*DICK launches into a soliloquy in an over-the-top Shakespearean style*) 'To be, or not to be: that is the question: Whether 'tis nobler in the mind to suffer the slings and arrows of outrageous fortune, or to take arms against a sea of troubles, and by opposing end them? To die: to sleep . . .' (*DICK takes low bow as GUV keenly applauds*)

GUV: Bravo! Well done, good and faithful employee.

NARRATOR: Finally Guv'nor called Harry to give an account.

HARRY: (*Looking sheepish*) Nice-ish to see you, Guv. Now before you say anything, if I'd been given what Tom and Dick were given, I would have done the same as them, probably better. But come on, a pair of shoes and a lousy thousand pounds. What was I supposed to do with that?

GUV: Well, I was hoping for something on the lines of you aiming at being England's new Linford Christie!

HARRY: Well, knowing what a hard taskmaster you are, I thought the safest thing was to bury it all where no harm could come to it. So here they are: the shoes are still brand new and not a single penny of the money is missing.

GUV: (*Takes goods, looks upset*) Go away from me, you wicked and lazy employee. (*HARRY slopes off, and freezes with his back to the audience*) Tom, you have proved yourself faithful in what I have given you. Perhaps you can use these too. (*Gives HARRY's gifts to TOM*)

TOM: Thanks, Guv.
NARRATOR: So, the moral of the story is this . . .
GUV: Whatever gifts God has given you . . .
TOM: Whether big or small . . .
DICK: Use them wisely and they will be multiplied.
HARRY: But misuse or neglect them and they will be
              taken away.
              (*Sketch closes with a second vocal trumpet
              fanfare. Freeze and fade to blackout*)

TEACHING POINT

Jesus teaches us that it doesn't matter what gifts we have.
What is most important is how we use them.

BIBLE REFERENCE

Matthew 25:14–30

(C) DEATH AND RESURRECTION

Kiss of Death

INTRODUCTION

Instead of the traditional portrayal of Judas as a tortured soul, this harsh piece gives no excuse for Judas' terrible betrayal of Jesus. Yes, Jesus knew that Judas was going to betray him, but more than being a puppet of God's will, Judas had freewill in his decision. The sketch reveals Judas as an embezzler who wanted political rebellion for his own greedy motives, with terrible consequences. Although the subject matter could be no more serious, the piece should be played with an element of black comedy as well as having a real sinister edge.

Characters: JUDAS; BENJAMIN, a tabloid journalist.

As the lights go up, we hear offstage whispering, occasionally the words 'Judas' and 'cheat' are audible. BENJAMIN is sitting at a table for two, looking around. As JUDAS enters, BENJAMIN calls him over and the offstage whispering stops.

BENJAMIN: Judas Iscariot . . . Over here, I've got you a coffee.

JUDAS: (*Agitated*) Keep your voice down, can't you? This is meant to be in confidence.

BENJAMIN: Ooohh! Keep your hair on. It was your suggestion to meet here. I ask you, Victoria Station of all places. (*Sips coffee*) Ugghhh! This coffee is absolutely foul. Ninety-nine pence each these cost me.

JUDAS: Ssshhh! Look, are you interested in this story, or not?

BENJAMIN: Well, that rather depends on you, buddy boy. If it's half as exciting as I think it could be, *The Daily Manure* will be willing to pay you a pile of money.

JUDAS: Good. Ever since I got involved with, er, our mutual friend, there's not been a sniff of the big money I was hoping for.

BENJAMIN: Bit money-hungry, aren't you, Mr Iscariot?

JUDAS: I only want what's coming to me.

BENJAMIN: Well come on then, what have you got for us?

JUDAS: What do you wanna know? I can give you the full inside story on the world's most wanted agitator – where he hangs out, who his allies are, how he shows up the nation's so-called religious leaders . . . Basically pal, I'm one of his closest friends and advisers. Whatever you and your sordid people want, I can get.

BENJAMIN: I hope you don't mind me asking you this, but if you're such a close mate, why are you dropping him right in the doodoo?

JUDAS: Why do you think? (*Rubs fingers together indicating money*)

BENJAMIN: Ah, back to the dosh, are we? Reports that I've read say you've already had your hand in the till, dipping into your pal's funds whenever it suited you.

JUDAS: (*Loses temper*) I earned that money! Would you work with someone for years with no payment?

BENJAMIN: No, Judas, I suppose I wouldn't. And I wouldn't expect you to work for me gratis neither. So here's the offer. First, I want your exclusive inside story, no holds barred. I wanna know everything – what he does, when, where and why. And second, I need you to hand him over to the authorities, at a set place and time, with me there of course, capturing it for posterity with my Canon Sureshot for a worldwide exclusive. For these services *The Daily Manure* will pay you the sum of £30,000. (*Holds up cheque*)

JUDAS: Thirty grand, eh!

BENJAMIN: That should compensate you for loss of earnings, with a very large bonus.

JUDAS: (*Takes cheque and shakes hands*) You have yourself a deal.

BENJAMIN: Lovely. So when can you arrange for us to do the business?

JUDAS: You know Speakers' Corner in Hyde Park? (*BENJAMIN nods*) Tomorrow night, 9 p.m. Bring the authorities. And your camera.

BENJAMIN: It's gonna be a bit on the dark side, isn't it? And your man keeps a low profile. How will we know which one he is?

JUDAS: (*Pause*) Tell you what. I'll walk up to him and greet him with a kiss.

BENJAMIN: Oh yes, I like that. Think of the headlines! 'Betrayed by a kiss' . . . 'Kiss of death'. I like it, Judas, very poetic. I like it a lot.

JUDAS: Keep it down. So, until nine o'clock tomorrow then.

BENJAMIN: Oh yes, nine o'clock tomorrow. We'll be there. (*JUDAS exits. BENJAMIN sips coffee*) Ugghhh! It really is absolutely disgusting. (*To audience*) Nearly as disgusting as I am. But I tell ya, it's not a patch on that filthy squealer. (*He laughs to himself as offstage whispers start again. They stop suddenly. Blackout*)

TEACHING POINT

When we fail to follow Jesus faithfully, our selfishness can have terrible knock-on effects.

BIBLE REFERENCES

Matthew 26:14–16, 47–50; John 6:70–71

The Last Temptation

INTRODUCTION

A highly controversial film, *The Last Temptation of Christ*, was released in 1988, and caused a furore among the Christian populace. This piece is, if you like, the Christian perspective on the theme of that film. While Christ was at his lowest ebb on the cross, separated from the Father, it gave Satan his last opportunity to tempt Christ off the cross, and change the course of history.

The use of percussion and music, live or pre-recorded, will certainly add to the effectiveness of this piece.

Characters: JESUS; SATAN; VOICE 1; VOICE 2; optional offstage crowd voices.

Lights slowly come up on JESUS who is standing centre stage. The audience do not see that his wrists are tied separately with two ropes, and are being held at stage left and right by VOICE 1 and VOICE 2. As JESUS begins to speak, the lights are only half up.

JESUS: (*Quietly*) My Father, if it is possible, let this cup be taken away from me. But I want your will to be done, not mine.

VOICES: (*Whispers slowly gain volume*) Crucify him, crucify him, crucify him . . . (*The words continue and slowly gain volume. They are then spoken in time to a beating drum. A loud drum beat and shout are heard as the lights go full up, and at the same time VOICE 1 and VOICE 2 pull hard on the ropes giving the image of Jesus on the cross. The following lines are spoken above crowd noises offstage and appropriate music and percussion*)

VOICE 1: Here, look at the sign: 'This is the King of the Jews'.

VOICE 2: Ooh yes, we salute you, Your Majesty.

VOICE 1: So you say you can destroy the temple and build it again in three days? (*Derisory laughter*)

VOICE 2: Well then, you better come down off the cross . . . if you're the Son of God that is . . . (*More laughter*)

VOICE 1: He was a clever clogs at saving others, but he can't save himself, can he?

VOICE 2: King of Israel, are you? Come down off the cross and we'll believe you.

VOICE 1: He's all talk and no action. Look at him.

VOICE 2: Pathetic, isn't it? Totally pathetic!
(*A loud drum beat. They all freeze in total silence. Out of the silence we hear slow hand-clapping and SATAN enters*)

SATAN: (*Clapping hands slowly*) Ignorant fools. They have no idea what or who they are dealing with. (*Looks at JESUS*) Do they? Jesus . . . Jesus . . . (*JESUS looks at him*) Ah, hello. I think you know who I am. In your time of deepest pain and loneliness I thought I'd come to you, in true friendship you understand. I sincerely mean that. I have the greatest respect for you. I see your fingers are free. You are able to move them, yes? Then why not click them, eh? You have the power. Just click your fingers and legions of angels will come down and rescue you. Believe me, you can finish this thing, this pain, and I know it hurts really bad. These ignorant fools don't deserve you; they reject you, they curse you. Come down. Come down and stand alongside me – the only one that's here in your hour of need. Everyone else, well, they've all disappeared. Come on, come down.

JESUS: (*Quietly*) No.

SATAN: Stubborn as ever. (*He turns from JESUS and sits on chair at the side of stage*) Let me tell you a little story. There was a man, a great man. He was well respected and loved, but his obsession with his spiritual deity spoiled the wonderful human being he undoubtedly was. The obsession nearly drove him to the most cruel death imaginable, but at the last moment, as if by a spark of true inspiration, he saw sense, saw what he was doing to these people around him who loved him, and so he decided to save his life and put an end to his childish obsession. Well, the people's love and respect for him grew, he was the Number One Guy. He fell in love with a beautiful woman, they had children, and those children grew up to love him and be like him. His life was inspirational, people were inexplicably drawn to him and his wonderful human qualities. You could even say he changed people's lives. He lived to a ripe old age and he died peacefully in his own bed, with those who loved him most all around him. What more could any man want? (*Turns to JESUS*) This could be your destiny . . . perfection.

JESUS: *Eloi, Eloi, lama sabachthani?* My God, my God, why have you forsaken me?

SATAN: (*Urgently*) He has . . . he has forsaken you. But I have not. Here I am. Come and stand alongside me. Come down. (*Shouts*) Come down!

JESUS: (*Stares at SATAN*) It is finished.

SATAN: No!
          (*As soon as this is spoken, we hear VOICES and crowd cry out loudly. The ropes are pulled tighter so that JESUS' body jolts and his head drops. SATAN falls to his knees in defeat. All of this should take only a few seconds, then we return to silence and stillness*)

SATAN: (*Quietly*) It is finished. (*Fade to blackout*)

TEACHING POINT

In our worst times of temptation, we can turn to Jesus for help. He has been through more than we could ever comprehend.

BIBLE REFERENCES

Matthew 4:1–11, 26:39, 27:35–53

Final Requests

INTRODUCTION

This short sketch for two males charts a possible interplay between the two thieves on either side of Jesus at the time of crucifixion. Luke's Gospel records that, in their last hours, one turned to Jesus while the other continued to scoff. The piece requires the audience to imagine Jesus in the middle of the thieves; and remember, at the beginning of the sketch, it may not be obvious to everyone watching exactly who the characters are.

Characters: THIEF ONE; THIEF TWO.

As the lights go up, we see THIEF ONE and THIEF TWO in positions of crucifixion. This should be suggested in a simple way, e.g. resting a plank of wood between the back of the neck and forearms. There is an empty space between them where Jesus would be.

ONE: (*Short period of tutting*) Pathetic. Absolutely pathetic.

TWO: Have you finished complaining? You're wearing me out.

ONE: (*Sarcastic*) Oh, I'm sorry. Flippin' 'eck, it's hard work hanging on these crosses!

TWO: I don't think the Roman authorities designed them for their comfort values.

ONE: You ain't kiddin' there, pal! (*Short pause*) Pathetic, isn't it? Absolutely pathetic.

TWO: Why don't you just shut up and leave him alone?

ONE: Well, all that rubbish he's been spouting on about being the Son of God – I don't hear him saying much about all that now. In actual fact, he hasn't said much at all, has he?

TWO: He can't get a word in edgeways.

ONE: Oh, ha ha!

TWO: Just let him die in peace.

ONE: (*Pause, then ONE looks towards Jesus who has apparently just spoken*) Did he just say something or am I imagining things?

TWO: Yeah, I think he did.

ONE: (*To Jesus*) Beg your pardon, mate? (*To TWO*) What did he say then?

TWO: I don't think you'll believe me if I tell you.

ONE: Come on, try me out.

TWO: I think he said, 'Father, forgive them, for they don't know what they are doing.'

ONE: (*Screams*) What? Don't know what they're doing? Yes they do, mate! They are letting us suffer the most undignified death imaginable. Forgive them? I know what I'd do to 'em given half a chance.

TWO: Yes, well, that's exactly why you've ended up here in the first place.

ONE: Thank you for reminding me. (*To Jesus*) If you are really the Messiah, stop playing about. Prove it by saving yourself – and while you're at it, you can save me too. Don't bother about him though, he's a right criminal!

TWO: Have you got no scruples at all?

ONE: No!

TWO: We deserve to die for what we've done. We can't have any complaints. But him, well, he hasn't done anything wrong.

ONE: Oh, boo hoo for him then! What's made you start

creeping around him all of a sudden? You thought he was as nutty as I did a few hours ago.

TWO: Well, I'm allowed to change my mind, aren't I?

ONE: Whatever you say.

TWO: (*To Jesus*) Jesus, will you remember me when you come into your kingdom?

ONE: (*Muttering*) Oh, that's all I need, two loonies. The sad, desperate plea of one dying man to another. Pathetic. (*To TWO*) Well, what did he make of your final request then?

TWO: He promised me that I'd be with him today in paradise.

ONE: (*Laughs*) Well, it's not really my idea of paradise, I must say. Still, each to his own.

TWO: Just a few more hours.

ONE: Blimey, it's got dark all of a sudden and it's only midday.

TWO: Yeah, you're right, it has. Pitch black. (*Sudden blackout*)

TEACHING POINT

We are saved by faith, not works – and it's never too late to ask for God's forgiveness.

BIBLE REFERENCE

Luke 23:39–44

The Why Files

INTRODUCTION

Predictably from the title, this piece is loosely based on the BBC TV series, *The X Files*. Sulker and Mouldy are paranormal experts working for Pilate, discussing the mystery surrounding the resurrection. Using music and costumes relating to the programme will add to the sketch. It can be used for a wide range of events as it requires no prior knowledge, and, importantly, introduces the key evidences for Jesus' resurrection.

Characters: SULKER; MOULDY.

From the darkness, we see two torch beams, shining into the audience. We also hear creepy music associated with The X Files. *Suddenly one of the beams dies, and we hear the conversation begin, still in the dark.*

SULKER: Oh, typical.

MOULDY: What's up?

SULKER: The batteries have gone on my flippin' torch.

MOULDY: I told you to buy Duracells, didn't I?

SULKER: Oh, shut up.

MOULDY: But oh no, you had to get the cheap Woolworth's own brand ones.

SULKER: Agent Mouldy, will you shut up! Anyway, it's probably only a loose connection. (*We hear shaking and banging of torch, followed by the return of the second beam*) Aha, see! Once again my world is illuminated. (*Lights slowly begin to come up*)

MOULDY: I'm so pleased for you, Agent Sulker. Now, do us a favour and shine your torch over here so I can read this file.

SULKER: (*Shines torch as indicated by MOULDY*) Oh, is it an X file?

MOULDY: No, it's a Why file.

SULKER: A Why file?

MOULDY: Yes, apparently our illustrious leader, Governor Pilate, has got a bit of a problem with a mysterious empty tomb. So, he's called in his crack team of highly trained paranormal operatives to find out why.

SULKER: Ooh, highly trained paranormal operatives. Who are they?

MOULDY: Us!

SULKER: Us? Oh no. We always get lumbered with all the manky jobs.

MOULDY: Oh stop sulking, Agent Sulker. This is a good case.

SULKER: (*Resigned*) Come on, then. Give us the background.

MOULDY: That's more like it. (*Reading from file*) Well, this guy Jesus, after a spell of preaching, teaching, performing miracles and claiming to be the Son of God, got himself in a bit of bother with the religious authorities, who, to cut a long story short, sentenced him to death.

SULKER: Yeah, skip all that bit. I read all about it in *The Jerusalem Herald.*

MOULDY: Well, after he died, he was buried in the tomb right behind us. (*They shine torches behind them, and look in tomb at rear centre of stage*) Three days later, we have one missing corpse, one empty tomb and one extremely panicky Governor Pilate.

SULKER: Pppff! They called us in for a simple one like this!

MOULDY: Ah, ah, ah! There is one more thing. Since the disappearance of the body, there have been dozens of sightings of Jesus around town, apparently looking in tip-top condition.

SULKER: (*Pause*) Ah, well, that puts a slightly different complexion on things. But, come on, Agent Mouldy, think rationally. Before we consider the paranormal, we need to eliminate the normal. There's a load of possible explanations.

MOULDY: Come on then. I'm all ears.

SULKER: Well, for a start, how do we know Jesus actually died?

MOULDY: Are you being serious?

SULKER: Every avenue should be explored, wouldn't you agree?

MOULDY: Yes, yes, I agree. We should examine this avenue most carefully. Well, for a start, he was flogged within an inch of his life. He was then nailed to a cross through his wrists and feet and left for six hours, and just for good measure he had a spear shoved in his side . . .

SULKER: Yeah, well . . .

MOULDY: Oh, there's more. If you still think he could survive that little lot, he then had to last out in a non-air-conditioned tomb without any water for a couple of days, remove layers of cloth soaked in gallons of spices, and then for his absolute *pièce de résistance*, shove away a stone that half a dozen gladiators would have struggled with.

SULKER: (*Pause*) Mmmm. So basically what you're saying is . . .

MOULDY: What I'm saying is, I think we can safely assume he died.

SULKER: Then he must have been removed.

MOULDY: Who by? Paul Daniels?

SULKER: Don't be stupid. Removed as in stolen.

MOULDY: Stolen! Well, I've heard of people nicking car stereos and VCRs, but who would want to steal a dead body?

SULKER: His disciples.

MOULDY: How did they manage that then, with a couple of burly security guards on twenty-four-hour watch?

SULKER: Well, I don't know. Maybe they arranged some kind of distraction. A couple of dolly birds with low-cut tops and ra-ra skirts.

MOULDY: Ra-ra skirts!

SULKER: You know what I mean. They distract the burly security guards, his followers come in from the other side, push away the stone and make off with the corpse.

MOULDY: Brilliant! Governor Pilate is currently concocting all manner of horrible deaths for his disciples, and they'd be willing to die knowing it was all some cock and bull story. I don't think so.

SULKER: Oh, you're always so negative.

MOULDY: That's 'cos your ideas are so downright stupid.

SULKER: Aha! I think I have it.

MOULDY: Here we go again.

SULKER: A government cover-up!

MOULDY: Oh, here goes Miss Paranoid.

SULKER: Come on Mouldy, you know what these government officials can be like. Yes, I bet they removed him to undertake some highly confidential experiments, or for political gain in the run-up to the next elections.

MOULDY: Hardly likely is it, bird brain?

SULKER: Why not?

MOULDY: If Governor Pilate is running around like a headless chicken trying to get answers, it's hardly likely he's nicked the body, is it? If he had, he'd produce it pretty sharpish to put an end to all the unrest and rumours.

SULKER: All right, clever clogs. So, let's recap then. We know Jesus definitely died and was put in the tomb under round-the-clock guard. The disciples couldn't have stolen him, and even if they could have, they wouldn't martyr themselves for a fairy story. And the government can't have anything to do with it or they would have let on by now, and nipped the rumours in the bud.

MOULDY: Precisely.

SULKER: So, Agent Mouldy, where exactly does that leave us?

MOULDY: In all honesty, Agent Sulker, I haven't got a clue. (*Lights begin to fade*) But I'll tell you what. The truth is out there!

SULKER: You're right this time. The truth is out there! (*Lights fade to blackout, leaving the torches shining as at beginning of sketch. Torches are switched off*)

TEACHING POINT

The Easter evidence points overwhelmingly to the resurrection miracle.

BIBLE REFERENCE

Mark 16:1–8

Pooper Scooper

INTRODUCTION

This monologue is ideal for any Easter setting. It imagines a possible thought process of Pilate, as he looks back on the Easter events. The piece requires little movement, but a strong actor will be needed to deliver the text well. Although there may be a couple of laughs early in the sketch, the overall aim is for a more serious and thought-provoking view of the story through the eyes of one of the key characters.

Character: PILATE.

There is a musical introduction as the lights go up. PILATE is sitting on a chair and is looking down. As the music comes to a sudden stop, he looks up quickly and addresses the audience.

PILATE: Of course I know what everyone calls me behind my back. 'Pilate, the pooper scooper'! Oh yes they do. Caiphas, Herod and all the other politicos. Pilate, the pooper scooper. And I suppose it's true really. Every time they need some poop cleared up, which is fairly often, they use me to scoop. To be honest, I don't mind. I mean, that's my job. Keeping them sweet, so they keep the people sweet, thus avoiding any unrest. Rome doesn't take too kindly to any rioting, as I've been warned on countless occasions. That's how politics works, and I've no real problem with it. Except for one particular instance last week . . .

I remember the day clearly, as the previous evening I'd been having trouble with Lady Procula, my beloved wife, about the toothpaste tube of all things! (*Mimics Lady Procula*) 'You think you're such a wonderfully clever man, who runs the country and can do as he pleases. But why, oh why, is it so difficult to squeeze the toothpaste tube from the bottom? Why must you squeeze it from the middle?' This had caused an atmosphere of unrest for the night, and to top it all, I was woken early the next morning by Caiphas and his cronies, who were declaring a state of national emergency downstairs. I went to see what the problem was. Caiphas was a mixture of viciousness and anxiety, somewhat reminiscent of a rottweiler on heat! (*Mimics Caiphas*) 'Governor Pilate, I need you to sign a death warrant immediately. This man here, Jesus of Nazareth, is causing riots against the government and claiming to be a messiah!' Caiphas is rather prone to exaggeration, so I asked the man he'd indicated if it was true. He simply said yes. I could tell straight away that this Jesus was not some seditious troublemaker, nor was he mad. In the face of all the hullabaloo surrounding him, he was totally calm. Totally sure of who he was, and what he was doing. I think it was a mixture of the man's obvious innocence, the previous evening's debacle with the toothpaste, and the fact that Caiphas had dragged me out of bed at such an obscene hour, that instead of just signing the warrant, as was my usual practice, I used some ruse that Jesus was a Galilean to pass the problem on to Herod. They took him away and I went back to bed. But I had the distinct feeling that this wasn't the last I would hear of Jesus of Nazareth. And I was dead right. Herod toyed around with him, couldn't find any reason for the death penalty, so sent him back to me, Pilate the pooper scooper!

(*Short pause with music. PILATE changes his position*)

I wanted to set him free, I truly did. I was just too much of a coward. The political pressure was too much to bear. You see, our nation has gone very PC – politically correct. It's not the done thing to claim you're the Son of God, even if it's true. During the hearing, Jesus just stood in silence, taking all the abuse. I said to him, 'Say something. Can't you hear all their accusations?' Nothing! What could I do? It's not my fault. It's very hard to defend a man who won't defend himself. I authorised a severe flogging as a kind of compromise. I'm not proud of it, but that's what we do in politics, compromise. He had no complaint as they took him away to literally tear the flesh from his back. But of course, this wasn't enough for them. My last attempt to set him free was an ancient custom, allowing me to release one prisoner to the people at this particular time of year. I offered them Jesus or Barabbas, a notorious murderer. Of course they'll choose Jesus, I thought. (*Shakes head*) So, now not only do I condemn the innocent, but also set free the obviously guilty. (*Picks up pace, agitated*) The crowd start shouting, 'Crucify him, crucify him!' And I ask them what crime he's committed. 'Crucify him, crucify him!' still louder. 'But there's no reason to sentence him to death,' I protest. 'Crucify him, crucify him!' (*Pause*) I have no words of defence left. I hand him over, and make a very public show of washing my hands, as if to say, 'It's not my responsibility. I don't care. Do what you want.' But I *do* care. My hands were clean, but not my heart. But I kept telling myself it was the correct political decision. I made my judgement, now I have to live with it. Well, what would you have done?

(*Short pause with music. PILATE changes his position*)

I watched the crucifixion incognito. The crowd baying for his blood, the same crowd incidentally who a few weeks ago were calling him Messiah! I blame them. The centurions who callously nailed him to the cross . . . I blame them. Caiphas and his corrupt council, laughing and jeering as another threat was silenced . . . I blame them. Me, the man who had the power to stop all this, the man who was too cowardly to stop all this, Pilate, the pooper scooper . . . above all, I blame him. (*Picks up newspaper*) And unless you've had your heads buried in the sand, I'm sure you've read all the headlines: 'Missing Messiah', 'King of the Jews' body stolen', 'Jesus risen from the dead, claim disciples'. It all leaves me with much food for thought. He certainly died, I saw it with my own eyes. So, did the disciples steal the body? Pretty impossible and even less likely. Our political opponents accuse us of hiding the body, which is totally ludicrous! If we could produce the body and end all the gossip, don't they think we would? Which leaves one option. That he did, in fact, as he said he would, rise from the dead. That he was, in fact, who he said he was, the Son of God. If it's true, then I condemned the Son of God to crucifixion. Will he ever forgive me? (*Slowly*) Will he ever forgive me? (*Music as lights fade to blackout*)

TEACHING POINT

We all have to answer for ourselves the question Pilate asked: 'What shall I do, then, with Jesus who is called Christ?'

BIBLE REFERENCES

Matthew 27:11–26; Luke 23

Walk the Talk

Christian Life and Lifestyle

Beef Stew Without Dumplings

INTRODUCTION

This sketch illustrates the famous biblical account of Jesus' visit to the home of Mary and Martha. The story lends itself wonderfully to comedy, with poor Martha getting increasingly frustrated at her sister's quiet stillness. Martha should be played with a degree of farce, as she rushes around fruitlessly preparing for Jesus' arrival.

Characters: MARY; MARTHA; JESUS.

MARY is sitting at a table with her eyes closed. MARTHA runs frantically from one side of stage to the other, cleaning, tidying, carrying, etc., giving MARY filthy looks. She starts to sweep up around Mary.

MARTHA: (*Sweeping furiously*) Are you all right there, Mary?

MARY: (*Unfazed*) Yes, thank you.

MARTHA: You're not wearing yourself out too much then?

MARY: No, I'm fine, thanks.

MARTHA: Oh that's good. Only I wouldn't want you to over-exert yourself!

MARY: Martha, why don't you sit down and have a rest? You've been darting around all day.

MARTHA: You don't think I enjoy running around like a crazy thing, do you? It's all very well you sitting around in a state of tranquil equilibrium,

140

	but that don't get the dinner cooked, you know.
MARY:	It doesn't matter, Martha. That's not what's important.
MARTHA:	That's not what's important, she says. Of course, if it was down to you, the place would look like a pigsty, and our VIP guest would be served up a plate of cordon bleu spaghetti hoops on toast! If you don't mind me saying, Mary, I don't think that's the kind of hospitality the Son of God would expect.
MARY:	Well, we'll soon find out. He's due anytime now.
MARTHA:	(*Panic-stricken*) What's the time then?
MARY:	About five to.
MARTHA:	*What?* (*Rushing offstage*) I haven't even started doing the dumplings yet. (*There is much clattering offstage then MARTHA reappears*) Where's the suet?
MARY:	What?
MARTHA:	Where's the suet? I can't make dumplings without any suet.
MARY:	I don't know. Maybe we've run out.
MARTHA:	Oh, what a total disaster! I wonder if Lazarus' convenience store is still open. He'll probably have some. What do you think?
MARY:	I don't know, Martha. I shouldn't worry about it. Just forget the dumplings.
MARTHA:	Forget the dumplings! Don't be so daft, Mary. I'm doing a beef stew. You can't have a beef stew without dumplings. That's like having lamb without mint sauce. Forget the dumplings! I'll go and have another look. (*MARTHA exits*)
JESUS:	(*Enters without MARY seeing*) Hello Mary.
MARY:	(*Jumps*) Oh, you made me jump. (*They greet each other*)

JESUS:	It's so lovely to see you, Mary. How are you feeling?
MARY:	Oh, OK. All the better for seeing you, Master.
JESUS:	Is Martha home? (*At this moment there is a huge clatter from offstage*)
MARTHA:	(*Shouting from offstage*) *Aaggghhh*! Mary! How many times have I told you about putting them pans away properly?
MARY:	(*Calmly*) Yes, she's just preparing us a meal.
MARTHA:	(*Enters with a saucepan on her head*) I could have had a nasty accident in . . . (*Tails off as she sees JESUS*) Oh, hello Master. You're very . . . punctual.
JESUS:	Hello Martha, it's lovely to see you. (*They greet each other*)
MARTHA:	(*Takes a duster from her pocket and dusts off chair*) Here you are, Master. Please take a seat.
JESUS:	Thank you, Martha. Are you going to come and join us?
MARTHA:	(*Generally digging at and hinting to MARY*) No, I'll just go and finish off the dinner . . . in the kitchen . . . on my own . . . without any help from anyone else whatsoever . . .
JESUS:	Is there anything wrong, Martha?
MARTHA:	No, nothing at all, I'm on top of the world. (*Short pause, then change of tone*) Well, yes, there is actually. I've been running around like a woman possessed, getting the house tidied, preparing the meal, all in time for your arrival. And Lady Muck here has been sitting there with her backside super-glued to that chair all day. I mean, it's not fair, is it? Can't you tell her to at least give me a hand with the dumplings?
JESUS:	No.
MARTHA:	Oh!

JESUS: I'm sorry to be so blunt, Martha, but I like Mary just where she is.

MARTHA: Well, I'm sorry to spoil your fun. I know my place, back in the kitchen . . .

JESUS: Wait a minute. Do you know what I'd like more than anything else at the moment?

MARTHA: Beef stew without dumplings, I hope.

JESUS: No. I'd like you to come and sit down, and give me the pleasure of your company.

MARTHA: (*Taken aback*) Oh! But what about the dinner?

JESUS: Don't worry about the dinner. I'm sure I'll enjoy whatever you give me.

MARY: Please, Martha. Come and sit with us.

MARTHA: Well, if you both really insist. It'll be nice to take the weight off my feet. (*She sits down. Pause as they all look at each other smiling. MARTHA eventually addresses JESUS*) Do you like spaghetti hoops on toast? (*Blackout*)

TEACHING POINT

As Christians, there are times when we need to be 'doing', to put our faith into action, and there are other times when we should concentrate on just 'being', quietly praying and listening to Jesus.

BIBLE REFERENCE

Luke 10:38–42

Alternative Lord's Prayer

INTRODUCTION

When we look seriously at the Lord's Prayer, it challenges us all about the things we do and say. In this sketch, the central character bares to God all her thoughts, openly and honestly. Young people will identify with Sammy, and she should be played with great warmth and humour. The sketch needs to be performed in the context of some teaching on the Lord's Prayer.

Characters: SAMMY, a teenage girl; VICAR; TWO GIRLS (non-speaking parts).

VICAR stands facing audience. The three girls are sitting on chairs facing the VICAR with their backs to the audience, as if they are the front row in class at school. SAMMY is in the middle. VICAR addresses the audience as if they are the rest of the school.

VICAR: OK now, shall we close the meeting with a word of prayer? Let's bow our heads . . . Our Father in heaven . . .

SAMMY: (*Turns around, looks up and addresses her inner thoughts to God. The VICAR and TWO GIRLS continue to hold their prayerful poses*) It's OK for you, God, nice and cosy up there. You should get a load of what I have to deal with!

VICAR: We honour your holy name . . .

SAMMY: Yes, we do, Lord, honest – well, most of the time

anyway. Must admit I do get a bit carried away sometimes, swearing and that, but I don't mean it nastily – not really . . .

VICAR: We ask that your kingdom will come now . . .

SAMMY: Well, maybe give it a few years, eh God? I mean, just enough time for me to get as famous as the Spice Girls,* so I can get to go out with some right hunk like David Beckham,* ooohh! Once I've done that, as far as I'm concerned, your kingdom can come as soon as you fancy.

VICAR: May your will be done here on earth, just as it is in heaven . . .

SAMMY: Yep, that's OK, just so long as it matches up with what I want and when I want it!

VICAR: Give us our food again today . . .

SAMMY: Oh yeah, definitely that one. I'm a right greedy mare me. (*Thinking deeply*) I wonder if they have any Burger Kings in heaven.

VICAR: Forgive us our sins . . .

SAMMY: Yes, please. And believe you me, there's plenty of them where I'm concerned.

VICAR: Just as we have forgiven those who have sinned against us . . .

SAMMY: Ah! Well, I don't think anyone, not even you, God, would expect me to forgive *her*. (*Indicates one of the other two girls*) Karen-Smelly-Ryan. Know what she did? Nicked my boyfriend, Darren Colman. Good luck to her anyway, he's a right div. But if she wants forgiving, she can forget it.

VICAR: Do not bring us into temptation . . .

SAMMY: No, you don't need to do that for me, God, I seem

---

* Replace with more appropriate topical reference as necessary.

	to do it quite well by myself, thank you very much.
VICAR:	But save us from the evil one . . .
SAMMY:	Well, if you're referring to old McHegarty, the maths teacher, definitely!
VICAR:	Yours, Lord, is the glory forever and ever. And we say together . . .
ALL:	Amen.
SAMMY:	Amen. That Lord's Prayer's right good, innit! (*Freeze and blackout*)

TEACHING POINT

A challenging look at our heart attitudes when our mouths are saying the familiar words of the Lord's Prayer.

BIBLE REFERENCE

Matthew 6:5–15

Wicked!

INTRODUCTION

People try all kinds of methods to pray impressively, but in Matthew chapter 6 Jesus teaches us that our quiet prayers, in the privacy of our own homes, are well rewarded. We don't need any particular structure or special holy words to gain his attention.

In this piece, Laura, a new convert, struggles to pray. Jesus is visible to the audience, but not to Laura. The actors should make the most of this dynamic, by at times getting so close that they nearly touch.

Characters: LAURA; JESUS.

We see two facing chairs. JESUS is standing with his back to the audience next to the right-hand chair. LAURA rushes in looking flustered.

LAURA: Oh no! I've gotta do it. Come on, Laura, you're a big girl now, this should be really easy. (*She tries to find a comfortable position to pray – standing with hands clasped, kneeling with elbows on chair, laying flat on floor, etc.*) Oh, I give up. It's impossible. (*She sits on left-hand chair*) When you become a Christian, they should give you lessons on how to pray. Instead, you're just thrown in at the deep end, totally clueless. (*Buries head in hands in total frustration*) Oh God!

JESUS: (*Sits down opposite LAURA*) Yes.

LAURA: (*Oblivious to JESUS*) Help me. How do I pray?

JESUS: It's easy really. Just tell me how you feel, tell me you love me, tell me what's on your mind, who and what you're worried about. But most importantly, listen to me. (*Leans in close to LAURA*)

LAURA: Not a word! I might as well be talking to a brick wall. Oh, I'm sorry. I don't mean that. I am trying, honest. I wish I could see you. (*She wanders around, then with a new sense of determination sits back down*) Right! (*She closes her eyes and clasps her hands*)

JESUS: Hello, I think we're in business.

LAURA: (*Religiously*) Oh heavenly Father, who art merciful unto thine own, hearken unto this unholy sinner . . .

JESUS: Oh no.

LAURA: I thanketh thee for thy covering in the holy sacrificial blood of the unblemished lamb, and I doth ask thy forgiveness of all my transistors . . . translators . . . transgressions . . . Oh . . . Amen!

JESUS: Oh dear, I think I doth need my seventeenth-century English dictionary. (*To audience*) It gets very confusing, you know. I have to know literally hundreds of languages, and then people will insist on using words from 400 years ago. The other day a young lad from Clapham was talking to me. He said, 'Jesus, you're wicked!' Well, of course, coming from a teenage lad in the millennium era, that's quite a compliment, but ten years ago . . . well, it would have had an entirely different meaning!

LAURA: (*Upset*) Oh!

JESUS: (*To audience*) Excuse me.

LAURA: Well, I made a right pig's ear of that, didn't I?

JESUS: Hey, come on, Laura. It was only your first effort. It gets easier as you go on, I promise. Now, calm down. (*LAURA does some deep breathing*) Now try again, but talk to me as you would to your friends, and leave out the Shakespearean stuff.

LAURA: (*Suddenly*) I've got a good idea. Why don't I forget all the Shakespearean stuff, and talk to you like a friend?

JESUS: (*Rolls eyes to audience*) Brilliant idea, Laura. Why didn't I think of that?

LAURA: I reckon this might work.

JESUS: Well, here we go!

LAURA: (*Heartfelt*) Jesus, where do I start? Thank you for listening to me and being patient with me . . . Thanks for loving me so much, and dying for me . . . I still haven't totally taken that in, but anyway . . . thanks for . . . well, thanks for so many things. I could sit here for hours reeling them all off . . . I pray for Mum and Dad, and my friends, especially Kim . . . I think they all reckon I'm a bit loopy going to church and all, but I pray that they'll . . . well, I don't know what I pray really, but just let it all be all right. I've got this feeling that keeping your standards is gonna be really hard, so I pray for your help to get me through it. I know I really wanna follow you, Jesus. It's not some teenage fad, like being obsessed with Boyzone.* I know what I want, whatever anyone else says. And I love you. Amen.

JESUS: (*Pause*) Thanks, Laura. That was lovely. Now it's important that you listen to me. I love you and I'll always be with you. Are you listening? I love you and I'll always be with you.

---

* Replace with more appropriate topical reference as necessary.

LAURA: Well, that felt much better. It's brill praying like that. Well, Jesus, I reckon we're gonna have some right good chats.

JESUS: (*Smiles*) Oh yes, Laura, I can assure you that we will. (*JESUS gets up and returns to his opening position, his back to the audience by the right-hand chair*)

LAURA: Oh, one more thing I've quickly got to tell you . . . You're absolutely and totally wicked! (*JESUS turns around with eyebrows raised to audience. Fade to blackout*)

TEACHING POINT

Jesus listens to our private and simple, heartfelt prayers. He wants us to be 'real' in prayer.

BIBLE REFERENCE

Matthew 6:5–8

A Prayer's Chance

INTRODUCTION

The Bible teaches us a lot about prayer, giving us guidelines on when, how and why we should pray. This sketch is a good way to lead into a talk or discussion on prayer; rather than examining the whys and wherefores, it challenges our motivations. The Bloggs family should be played in a highly stylised fashion. Master Bloggs, unlike the rest of his family, is highly intelligent.

Characters: MR BLOGGS; MRS BLOGGS; MASTER BLOGGS; MISS BLOGGS.

The lights come up on the Bloggs' front room. The action centres around their weekly ritual of watching the National Lottery draw. The scene opens with all the characters standing in front of their chairs, frozen.

MR:	Mr Bloggs. (*He sits*)
MRS:	Mrs Bloggs. (*She sits*)
MASTER:	Master Bloggs. (*He sits*)
MISS:	Miss Bloggs. (*She sits*)
MR:	It's Saturday night, it's ten to eight.
ALL:	(*Jump up*) Yeah!
MRS:	Tickets at the ready. It's a rollover jackpot week.
ALL:	Yeah!
MASTER:	Bob Monkhouse*, national treasure and comedy genius.

---

* Change name as appropriate.

151

ALL:	Yeah!
MISS:	Ladies and gentlemen, the one and only National Lottery!
ALL:	Yeah! (*All sit down*)
MRS:	Shut up, Mr Bloggs, it's about to start. Ooh, is it Arthur's turn this week or Guinevere's?
MR:	Arthur! That's what I like to see. I prefer Arthur. Oh look here, it's this week's celebrity starter coming up. Who's it gonna be? (*Pause*)
MR/MRS/MASTER:	(*Together*) Noel Edmonds. Uugghhh!
MISS:	Who's he when he's at home?
MR:	Are you thick, Miss Bloggs? Don't you know nuffin? He's the leader of the Conservative Party.
MRS:	Shut up, you two, and concentrate. Noel's about to get Arthur started up. (*All freeze staring at screen, humming opening of* Chariots of Fire *theme*)
MR:	Number four. (*Freeze breaks*) Yes, it's my beautiful number four. It always comes up. You know why I chose it? I took the date of my mum's birthday, the fourteenth, and minused it from the date of yours, darling, the twentieth, and hey presto!!
MASTER:	That makes six, Mr Bloggs.
MR:	What?
MISS:	The second number's coming up. It's . . . thirteen. Anybody got it?
MR:	Course we ain't got it, it's unlucky, innit?
MRS:	(*Smiling*) Well, it is if you didn't choose it, you silly superstitious

sausage. I don't go in for that super-
stitious rubbish myself.

MASTER: Here's the next one . . . thirty-nine.

MRS: Ooh, my age.

MR: Ha!

MISS: Have you got it, Mrs Bloggs?

MRS: No. Mystic Meg says it's unlucky to
choose your own age.

MR: Hypocrite! What's this? Look at that.
Thirty-eight! The flippin' machine's
on the blink. It should shake 'em up
a bit more. Thirty-nine, then thirty-
eight. Get the ref in, it's bloomin'
ridiculous.

MISS: I take it you haven't got thirty-eight
then, Mr Bloggs?

MR: No!

MASTER: Anyway, Mr Bloggs, the machine's
not on the blink. There's an equal sta-
tistical probability of the number
next to the previous one coming out,
as any other number.

MR: What on earth are you going on
about? What's statistics when they're
at home?

MASTER: You know, statistics . . . (*MR
BLOGGS looks confused*) Statistics is
the science concerned with the collection, classification and interpretation
of quantitative data, and with the
application of probability theory to
the analysis and the estimation of
population parameters. (*The others
stare at MASTER BLOGGS in disbelief*)

MR:	Yeah, well . . . what's the next number then?
MISS:	It's already gone up. Thirty-five.
MR/MRS:	(*Together*) Thirty-five! Yeesss!
MISS:	You both got it then?
MRS:	Course we 'ave, darling. It's the year the king was born.
MR/MRS:	(*Singing loudly*) 'Wise men say, only fools rush in, but I can't help falling in love with you.'
MR:	Yes, Elvis Aaron Presley, the king of rock 'n' roll. 1935 to 1977.
MASTER:	You can't have seventy-seven though, Mr Bloggs – it only goes up to forty-nine.
MR:	Ah yes, but that's why I do sixteen, 'cos it's seven plus seven . . . (*He smiles with his thumb up*)
MRS:	Come on boys, concentrate. It's the last number and we've both got two already, sweetheart.
MR:	Concentrate? Who d'ya think you are? Uri Geller? Come on everybody, quick, let's pray! One more number and we're lottery winners.
MISS:	Mr Bloggs, even if it comes up, you'll only have three numbers.
MR:	I don't care, missy, it's a matter of pride. I'm the only one in the factory who's never won. Every Saturday I've sat here since the flamin' thing started, and not once have I won, not a dicky bird. So pray!
MASTER:	But Mr Bloggs, it's only a tenner!
MR:	I don't care. Pray!

MRS:	Ooh, it's taking a long time for this last number to come up, innit?
MR:	Yes darling, it's called dramatic licence. Now, shut up and pray. (*They all put hands together and close eyes*)
MR:	(*Stands*) Dear God, please let one of my numbers come up, so I can be a lottery winner, one of the chosen people. Amen.
MRS:	(*Stands*) Dear God, for the sake of peace, I pray that one of his numbers comes up and not mine, otherwise we'll never hear the end of it. Amen.
MISS:	(*Stands*) Dear God, I pray that Sharon-Cowface-Bennett gets dumped by Alastair Johnston, so I can try and get off with him at the party next week. Amen.
MASTER:	(*Stands*) Dear God, I pray from the bottom of my heart for world peace, and an end to poverty and starvation. I also pray that (*enter local football team*) will win the league this season. Amen.
MR:	Don't push your luck, son. (*They all sit*)
MRS:	Oh, it's a waste of time, love. God don't listen to them sort of prayers.
MR:	Course he does, that's what he's there for – to give us what we want, when we ask.
MISS:	He's not a fruit machine, Mr Bloggs! Bung in a prayer, and get out what you ask. Everyone would be asking

	for a million pounds.
MR:	Yeah, well, that's just plain greed. (*All look at him accusingly*) Oh flippin' 'eck, I only want a tenner.
MASTER:	Surely, in generosity you pray for others, and then good things come to you anyway.
MR:	Well, I dunno about that, but my old man always told me you don't get nuffink in this world unless you ask for it.
MRS:	(*Holier than thou*) Not in this world, but maybe in another.
MR:	(*Snaps*) Oh, don't go all holy and religious on me, love.
MRS:	You were the one who insisted we all pray.
MR:	Oh, all right, just forget about it. (*Pause*) When do we pray then? Why do we pray?
MISS:	Last number's coming up. (*All freeze and hum* Chariots of Fire *theme*)
MR:	(*He breaks from freeze and clicks fingers to try and wake the others. They remain frozen. He then addresses the audience*) I suppose you all wanna know if my number's come up. Well tough! The sketch has gotta end somewhere, ain't it? (*He also freezes, then blackout*)

TEACHING POINT

Jesus teaches us that at the heart of prayer should be our love for him first, then others, then ourselves.

BIBLE REFERENCES

2 Chronicles 7:14; Matthew 6:33

Kids' Talk

INTRODUCTION

In the Bible, Jesus has much to say about children, and about how important they are to him. Our faith should always be child-*like*, but as we grow older, we should leave our child*ish* nature behind us, and become good examples for the rising generation. This sketch, although rather exaggerated, demonstrates this teaching.

Characters: BOY 1; BOY 2; DAD 1; DAD 2.

Lights come up on BOY 1 and BOY 2 centre stage.

BOY 1:	I've got a new Play Station.
BOY 2:	Who cares, so have I!
BOY 1:	Yeah, but I've got six new games *and* the Goldeneye gun . . .
BOY 2:	Big deal. I've got the rumble pack and fifteen games including Horrific Mortal Death Crypt 4, which cost £54.99.
BOY 1:	(*Blows raspberry*) Don't care.
BOY 2:	Yes you do.
BOY 1:	Don't.
BOY 2:	Do.
BOY 1:	Don't.
BOY 2:	*Yes you do!* (*Pause*) We've got a brand new Nicam stereo TV.
BOY 1:	Well, our video's brand new too.
BOY 2:	Whoopee doo! Bet your TV isn't as big as

ours, though.

BOY 1:	I bet it is.
BOY 2:	Bet it isn't. How big is yours then?
BOY 1:	Not telling ya . . .
BOY 2:	(*Taunting*) Ha, that's 'cos it's so titchy. (*Pause*) Well, I think ours is probably about a mile long.
BOY 1:	Duuurrrrr! It can't be a mile long or it wouldn't fit in your house, thicko!
BOY 2:	(*Defensively*) Well, it didn't fit in our house actually. My dad had to build an extension to fit it in.
BOY 1:	No he didn't!
BOY 2:	(*Increasing the volume*) Did.
BOY 1:	Didn't.
BOY 2:	Did.
BOY 1:	Didn't
BOY 2:	*Did!*
BOY 1:	*Didn't!*
DAD 1:	(*Charges in from stage left*) Will you boys please be quiet!
BOY 1:	Oh Dad, he started it.
BOY 2:	No I didn't, it was him.
BOY 1:	Him.
BOY 2:	Him.
BOY 1:	*Him!*
BOY 2:	*Him!*
DAD 2:	(*Charges in from stage right*) That's enough, you two!
BOY 2:	But Dad . . .
DAD 2:	*Enough!* Now calm yourself down and stop being so childish. (*To DAD 1*) Hello, John.
DAD 1:	Hello, Charles. Sorry about all their noise.
DAD 2:	Oh, no problem. Kids will be kids. (*Both laugh*) . . . Yes . . . Work going well, is it?

DAD 1:   Yeah, fantastic. The UK sales force have had a 68 per cent increase in profit.

DAD 2:   Great. Our UK sales are up 73 per cent.

DAD 1:   And how about exports?

DAD 2:   (*Smugly*) They're up 49 per cent too.

DAD 1:   (*Quickly*) Well, ours are up 59 per cent.

DAD 2:   So what? We've all just got a cash bonus.

DAD 1:   So have we.

TOGETHER: How much is yours?

DAD 1:   You first.

DAD 2:   No, you first.

DAD 1:   You.

DAD 2:   You.

DAD 1:   *You*!

DAD 2:   *You*!

DAD 1:   (*Sulky*) If you must know, it's two thousand pounds.

DAD 2:   Ha! Ours is three thousand.

DAD 1:   Well, I couldn't care less 'cos we're getting brand new company cars.

DAD 2:   Us too. We're getting BMWs.

DAD 1:   Us too. What series BMWs?

DAD 2:   Six.

DAD 1:   Ha! We're getting seven.

DAD 2:   *Double ha*! We're getting series nine really, I was only lying to you before!
                (*During this interplay, the boys have been sitting quietly at the side of the stage, looking at their dads in a confused kind of disgust*)

BOY 1:   Dad. . . . .

DAD 1:   Shut up! Don't interrupt! Can't you see Daddy's having a serious conversation? (*Freeze, then fade to blackout*)

TEACHING POINT

The need for adults to be positive role models for children and young people.

BIBLE REFERENCES

Proverbs 22:6; Matthew 18:1–6; 1 Corinthians 13:11

Honest Harry

INTRODUCTION

What is the most important thing or person in our lives? Jesus wants us to root out anything that could cause a block between ourselves and him. In this sketch, Honest Harry is confronted with the one thing that he puts above following Jesus, and is challenged to give it up. The sketch should be used in conjunction with a talk on priorities and the advantages of seeking first God's kingdom. The Posh Spice* poster at the centre of the sketch can be substituted with a signed England football or anything more appropriate.

Characters: JESUS; HARRY.

JESUS is seated centre stage, eyes closed in deep thought. HARRY enters and slowly approaches JESUS.

HARRY: (*Quietly*) Excuse me, sir. Hello! (*JESUS opens his eyes*) I'm sorry to interrupt your train of thought, but could I just shake your hand?

JESUS: (*Smiles*) Of course you can. (*They shake hands*) It's lovely to meet you, Harry.

HARRY: (*Shocked*) How do you know my name?

JESUS: Oh, don't worry about it, I just know these things. Now what is it I can do for you?

---

* Replace throughout with more appropriate topical reference if necessary.

HARRY: Well, I've just heard you speak, and I thought it was absolutely amazing. In actual fact, I think it's changed my life.

JESUS: Well, thanks Harry. I truly hope it has.

HARRY: Yes, I want to follow you from now on. I want to make sure I go to heaven. How can I do that?

JESUS: Well, you're a clever man, Harry. I'm sure you know the commandments. You mustn't murder . . .

HARRY: Never, sir! I wouldn't. I couldn't. You see, I'm a pacifist. I even get upset if I accidentally step on a creepy-crawly.

JESUS: Neither can you commit adultery.

HARRY: No sir, I would not! My Josephine is the most beautiful woman I know (barring Posh Spice,* of course). I love and honour her. I could never betray her.

JESUS: Well, that's good. How about the laws concerning cheating, lying and stealing?

HARRY: Hand on my heart, Lord. Never once have I broken any of those laws. I run a genuine business – you could ask anybody. They all call me Honest Harry. You do believe me, don't you?

JESUS: Oh yes, Harry, I do. I know you're telling the truth. Tell me, though, you're quite a rich man, aren't you?

HARRY: Well yes, I've been lucky. The business has earned me a fair few bob. Well, a fair few million bob to be precise.

JESUS: Well, I may need you to donate a large sum to charity to help those less fortunate than yourself.

HARRY: Not a problem. I already give to charitable causes.

---

* Replace as necessary.

But if you think I should up the amount, I'd be only too pleased. Just name your price.

JESUS: Well, how about your top-of-the-range Ferrari?

HARRY: My F . . . F . . . Ferrari? Ooh, now you are driving a hard bargain. Mind you, I suppose we are talking eternal life here. You gotta deal, Lord, and may I say how much I'm looking forward to following you for all eternity.

JESUS: (*Refers to little black book*) Aha!

HARRY: What's up? Is there a problem?

JESUS: Well, it seems like there's just one more little thing.

HARRY: Anything you want, Lord. What's mine is yours.

JESUS: I'll need your personally signed poster of Posh Spice.*

HARRY: (*Shocked*) Oh no! Anything but that. You can have the car, the house, anything. But that's my most prized possession. (*Dreamily*) I got that when I met her at *Top of the Pops* last year. It's got on it 'For dear Honest Harry, my number one fan. Lots of love and kisses, Posh Spice'.* Please, Lord, is there no other way?

JESUS: (*Shakes head*) I need to know that nothing in your life is more important than following me.

HARRY: (*Shakes JESUS' hand*) It's been a pleasure to meet you, Lord. Maybe another time, eh? (*HARRY exits*)

JESUS: Yes . . . maybe. (*JESUS closes his eyes. Fade to blackout*)

TEACHING POINT

We need to make following Jesus the number one priority in our lives.

---

* Replace as necessary.

BIBLE REFERENCE

Mark 10:17–22

Loadsalove

INTRODUCTION

So much has been written about love – not surprising as it is
right at the centre of Jesus' teaching. The idea of this sketch
is to show the sometimes fickle nature of human love compared to the depth and constancy of Jesus' love for mankind.
The actor playing Jesus also acts as a narrator, and the actors
playing the man and woman break into a variety of mini-
sketches using different characters, demonstrating aspects of
human love. The overall effect is comedic, with a serious
challenge at the end.

Characters: JESUS; MAN; WOMAN.

*MAN and WOMAN are sitting on chairs or a sofa. JESUS
stands behind.*

MAN:	(*Slushy*) I love you.
WOMAN:	(*Slushy*) I love you too.
MAN:	You're my precious schnooky lumps.
WOMAN:	(*Giggles*) You're my scrumptious honey bun.
MAN:	(*To audience*) I love her.
WOMAN:	(*To audience*) I love him.
BOTH:	(*Together*) We wanna be . . . *together*!
MAN:	I love you more.
WOMAN:	No, I love you more.
JESUS:	I love you most. (*MAN and WOMAN freeze*) What is true love? Love is patient and kind.

(MAN and WOMAN break from freeze. WOMAN stands to side of stage, MAN remains seated)

MAN: For goodness' sake, woman, get a shift on!

WOMAN: Hold yer horses, will ya!

MAN: Hold me horses! I've been sitting here holding 'em for the last two hours!

WOMAN: Well, you don't wanna spend the evening with me looking like a right old trout, do you?

MAN: There won't be any of the flippin' evening left by the time you get your backside out of the bathroom. How much make-up are you trowelling on, anyway?

WOMAN: Oh, calm down, Peter. Remember, patience is a virtue not a vice.

MAN: How many times have I told you, Maureen, I've got no time for patience. *(They freeze)*

JESUS: Love is never jealous or envious.
(MAN and WOMAN break from freeze. They are both seated, MAN is smiling at someone)

WOMAN: *(Hits man)* What are you playing at?

MAN: What?

WOMAN: I saw you.

MAN: Saw what?

WOMAN: Oh, 'ark at Mister Innocence. I saw you smiling and giving the eye to that young bit of stuff over there.

MAN: Oh rubbish, I was just being pleasant.

WOMAN: Oh, pleasant he calls it. Rolling his eyes and all sorts!

MAN: I was not rolling my eyes. Someone smiles at me, I return the gesture.

WOMAN: Yeah, you return the gesture if she's young and attractive. It's a different story if she's a right old battleaxe!

MAN: Well, I smile and gesture at you sometimes, don't I?

WOMAN: (*Offended*) Oh! (*They freeze*)

JESUS: Love is not easily angered. (*MAN and WOMAN break freeze*)

WOMAN: What time do you call this then?

MAN: I know. I'm sorry.

WOMAN: I suppose you've been having a booze after work.

MAN: No, the European contract was confirmed this afternoon, and we all had to stay on for a couple of hours.

WOMAN: Oh charming! It's nice to know you put a bunch of foreigners before me!

MAN: Darling, it really couldn't be helped.

WOMAN: Well, the microwave pizzas are in the freezer. Help yourself.

MAN: Please calm down, love.

WOMAN: Agh! If there's one thing that gets my goat, it's you telling me to calm down. (*They freeze*)

JESUS: It is not irritable or touchy.
            (*MAN and WOMAN break freeze. MAN starts to annoyingly flick WOMAN's ear*)

WOMAN: Will you stop it!

MAN: What! I didn't do anything. (*He flicks her ear again*)

WOMAN: Will you stop being so irritating!

MAN: Oooohhh! Touchy!

JESUS: It always perseveres.

MAN: (*Flicks her ear again. WOMAN looks annoyed. They freeze*)

JESUS: It does not count up wrongs.

WOMAN: (*Breaking from freeze*) That's seventy-four times in the last month I've had to tell you. (*Shouts*) Put the seat down! (*Freeze*)

JESUS: It is never rude.

MAN/WOMAN: (*Together they break freeze and blow raspberries at each other. Freeze*)

JESUS: It does not hold grudges.
(*MAN and WOMAN break freeze. They are now old age pensioners, so speak falteringly*)

WOMAN: Are you all right, Arthur?

MAN: Aye, not so bad.

WOMAN: Looks like there's something on your mind.

MAN: I were just recalling a low point in our relationship.

WOMAN: Oh, when were that, my lovely?

MAN: Back in 1946. I can even remember the date, January the eighth.

WOMAN: It don't ring no bells with me.

MAN: Nay, it wouldn't, but I'll tell ye, I'll never forget it. We were headed out to see the new Humphrey Bogart film at the Roxy, and you went charging by me, stomped right on my big toe, and never stopped to say sorry.

WOMAN: Yeah, and what next?

MAN: Next? There ain't no next. You bruised me toe and never said sorry. I tell ye, Agnes, I'll never forget it.

WOMAN: You remember that from over fifty years ago? Well, I hate to admit my mother were right, but when she called you a

	small-minded ninny, she were spot on! (*They freeze*)
JESUS:	Love is never selfish. (*MAN and WOMAN now break freeze and become young children*)
MAN:	It's my turn to play with the Laa-Laa doll. You had it all day yesterday.
WOMAN:	Ooohh, you fibber! You had Laa-Laa yesterday, so you get Dipsy today.
MAN:	Liar! I'm telling Mum. (*Calls out*) Mum! She's stolen my Teletubby. Laa-Laa's mine. (*MAN jumps and grabs one of JESUS' arms, who now becomes a doll. WOMAN grabs other arm and they have a tug of war*)
WOMAN:	Laa-Laa's mine!
MAN:	Mine! (*Repeat, rising to a crescendo*) (*After a short tug of war contest, MAN and WOMAN let go of JESUS' arm and he's left standing in the position of the cross. Silent pause and freeze. They both look towards him*)
JESUS:	Greater love has no one than this, that one lay down his life for his friends.
MAN:	I love you.
WOMAN:	I love you too.
MAN:	I love you more.
WOMAN:	No, I love you more.
JESUS:	I love you most. (*Freeze and blackout*)

TEACHING POINT

Jesus' demonstration of love is the greatest there has been, or ever will be.

BIBLE REFERENCES

John 15:13; 1 Corinthians 13:1–13

The Expected Thieves

INTRODUCTION

It always amazes me when people claim to know the date and time of Jesus' return. The Bible states clearly that only God the Father knows, not even Jesus, so I think it's highly unlikely that some guy with a prophecy about the Second Coming is ever going to be right.

In this short and rather silly sketch based on Jesus' teaching in Luke chapter 12, two bumbling thieves demonstrate what a nonsense it would be for Jesus to announce the time of his return. The two actors should really play this one for laughs, and the piece will need to be supported by some form of teaching.

Characters: BILLY; GEOFF.

BILLY and GEOFF tiptoe in, wearing traditional burglar costumes and holding swag-bags. They each carry a torch.

        (*BILLY drops torch*)

GEOFF: Ssshhhh!

BILLY: Sorry.

GEOFF: You are a bungling oaf!

BILLY: It was an accident. I said I was sorry.

GEOFF: Look at us! I mean, what do we look like?

BILLY: You told me to get some clothes suitable for doing a burglary job.

GEOFF: Yeah, but I didn't expect you to go to a fancy dress shop, did I? Look at us. We don't exactly blend into the crowd, do we?

BILLY: No, but think about it . . . wearing this, who in their right minds would think we really was robbers, eh?

GEOFF: Mmmm, well, I suppose I can see your point in a ridiculous kind of way. Come on then, let's see what we can half-inch in here.

BILLY: (*Steps forward and stubs his toe*) Ooww! Oh my toe, I think I've busted my toe.

GEOFF: Ssshhh! Keep it down, dopey! You'll have the whole house up.

BILLY: Oh, calm down. It don't matter anyway.

GEOFF: What do you mean it don't matter?

BILLY: I mean they know we're coming.

GEOFF: (*Jumpy*) What! Have they seen us through a window or something?

BILLY: No, I sent 'em a little note.

GEOFF: (*Pause, in shock*) You *what*?

BILLY: I sent 'em a note.

GEOFF: (*In disbelief*) Why?

BILLY: Well, I thought it was the decent thing to do really. If we're gonna make off with all their trinkets and valuables, I thought the very least we could do was let them know when.

GEOFF: You great big brainless buffoon!

BILLY: Don't be so ungrateful. Just think – now they know we're coming, they might've left everything handy for us. They may have even let their kids leave us a cookie and tumbler of whisky out before they went to bed.

GEOFF: Yeah, and they may also have left a couple of burly coppers on the other side of that door, ready to drag us down the nick!

BILLY: (*Pause for thought*) Fair point. I admit I hadn't considered that particular eventuality. So, in a case scenario like this, what would you suggest?

GEOFF: Well, my suggestion would be a speedy exit stage
             left.

BILLY: Mmmm, agreed. (*They exit stage left speedily.*
             Blackout)

TEACHING POINT

No one knows the time of Jesus' return, but we should be
prepared for it to happen at any time.

BIBLE REFERENCE

Luke 12:39

Tongues on Fire

INTRODUCTION

The two main characters in this sketch are a couple who constantly argue, and, as is revealed, always for absolutely ridiculous reasons. One of the central messages of the New Testament is the importance of loving our neighbour and building each other up as opposed to constantly arguing and using our tongues to tear each other apart. This is eloquently communicated in the passage found in James 3:3–12. I have used dramatic licence to bring Jesus into this sketch, to speak what I believe his message is to us today. To keep the football analogy, another major championship will have to be used if it's not a World Cup year!

Characters: MAN; WOMAN; JESUS (who acts as a referee).

MAN stands frozen by a chair, WOMAN is also frozen sitting on a chair. JESUS stands frozen at back of stage between them holding a whistle. We hear a single blast of the whistle, then all three clap familiar football chanting rhythm, and shout out 'Round One'. This is followed by a second blast of the whistle which acts as a starting-gun for the argument to begin. The row must be quick-fire for the piece to maintain pace.

MAN: Well, thank you very much.
WOMAN: What's your problem?
MAN: What's my problem, she says.
WOMAN: Sorry, love, but what are you going on about?
MAN: Oh, don't come the innocent with me, love.

175

WOMAN: I'm not 'coming the innocent' at all. I just
don't know what you're getting all steamed up
about.

MAN: I'm not getting all steamed up. I've got a justified
complaint!

WOMAN: Well, come on then, out with it.

MAN: You want me to spell it out?

WOMAN: *Yes*!

MAN: All right then. Well, I've been in there.

WOMAN: You've been in there. And where is that exactly?

MAN: (*Mimics*) Where is there exactly? Huh! The
bedroom, that's where.

WOMAN: Well, that must have been a novel experience for
you. And what is it in the bedroom that's
incensed you so?

MAN: You really don't know.

WOMAN: *No*!

MAN: Well, what new addition have I made to the
bedroom in the last couple of weeks?

WOMAN: You've got me there.

MAN: Oh, come on, woman, it's three foot by two foot,
multi-coloured and stuck on the wall.

WOMAN: Oh, *that*.

MAN: Yes, *that*. My World Cup wallchart.* Pathetic as
I know you think it is, I like it. At a moment's
glance, I can see who's playing who, when and
where, and what TV channel it's on. Now I
know you're not over-struck on it, but I didn't
think having it up for a month was asking too
much.

WOMAN: Well, I admit I don't think it adds much to the
overall ambience of the room, but I've already

---

* Replace with more topical reference as necessary.

said I don't mind you having it up. I still don't
see what your problem is.

MAN: Oh, you don't. Well, let me enlighten you. I've
just gone in there to fill in this afternoon's score,
like I always do as soon as I get home from
work, and what do I see?

WOMAN: (*Penny has dropped*) Oh!

MAN: Yes. Oh!

WOMAN: Look, I happened to see the result on the early
evening news so I thought I might as well fill the
score in for you.

MAN: Ha! I see. No remorse. It's *my* chart. *I* fill it in! I
was going to pass that on to my firstborn son as
a family heirloom and now you've totally ruined
it!

WOMAN: Oh, don't exaggerate. I haven't ruined it. The
score was 1-1. It looks just the same as if you'd
filled it in. No one will know the difference.

MAN: I will! Every time I look at it now, it'll scream out
at me: (*Shouts*) Austria 1, Chile 1* – You didn't
fill this score in!

WOMAN: Oh, stop being so pathetic.

MAN: I might as well burn it now. It's so typical of you.
You ruin everything.
(*We hear a blast on the whistle and they freeze.
This is followed by the same clapping football
chant followed by a shout of 'Round Two'. A
second blast of the whistle breaks the freeze again.
The action has changed: this time MAN sits and
WOMAN stands; she is now shouting at him. The
pace should still be fast*)

WOMAN: Well, thank you very much.

---

* Replace as appropriate.

MAN: What's your problem?

WOMAN: What's my problem, he says.

MAN: Sorry, love, but what are you going on about?

WOMAN: Oh, don't come the innocent with me, love.

MAN: I'm not 'coming the innocent' at all. I just don't know what you're getting all steamed up about.

WOMAN: I'm not getting all steamed up. I've got a justified complaint!

MAN: Well, come on, out with it.

WOMAN: You want me to spell it out?

MAN: Yes!

WOMAN: All right then. Well, I've been in there.

MAN: You've been in there. Well, where is that exactly?

WOMAN: (*Mimics*) Where is that exactly? Huh! The toilet, that's where.

MAN: The toilet. Well, sorry if I'm missing the point, my love, but you going to the loo is not really earth-shattering front-page news.

WOMAN: Oh, very funny, you are the epitome of wit!

MAN: What?

WOMAN: Look, am I not a tolerant woman?

MAN: Yes, darling, always.

WOMAN: Have I not willingly become a World Cup* widow?

MAN: Your selfless generosity has exceeded the expectations of any reasonable man.

WOMAN: Do I complain when you constantly watch matches, day in, day out? When you invite carloads of loutish cretins round, whose stench of lager, kebabs and fags drowns out even my most potent air freshener?

---

* Replace as appropriate.

MAN: No, darling. But what's any of this got to do with you going to the loo?

WOMAN: I'm just getting there! I can put up with all these major inconveniences, being as it's only for a month, but when I go to the loo and see that . . . well, I think it's positively past the limit.

MAN: See what exactly, love?

WOMAN: The toilet seat up, that's what! Why is it so flippin' difficult for you blokes to simply place it back down after you've finished? And what's wrong with all your aims? Thank goodness you're not playing for England.* You're even less on target than they are. They should have compulsory lessons for boys at school: 'How to go to the toilet in a civilised society'. It's absolutely disgusting.
              (*We hear three blasts of the whistle. On the first they freeze, and on the third they both turn and stand facing towards JESUS*)

JESUS: Now look here, you two. What is this arguing about? I'm sure that World Cup* wallcharts and toilet seats are really important to you, but in the whole scheme of things – well, I have to say they don't play a particularly key role. I know you both really love each other, and I also know deep down you realise that these arguments are a waste of time. So, yes, you can use your tongues to scream at and abuse each other, that's your free choice, but you could also use them to make each other feel really good. I'm not forcing you to do anything you don't want to do. It's just a thought.

---

* Replace as appropriate.

(*JESUS blows the whistle followed by the football clapping chant rhythm and a shout of 'Round Three'. A second whistle breaks the freeze and MAN and WOMAN turn to each other*)

MAN/WOMAN: (*Together*) Darling, I'm sorry . . .

MAN: Oh, you go first.

WOMAN: No, please, you go first.

MAN: No really, I insist you go first.

WOMAN: (*Getting annoyed*) In these instances, it's always the woman that goes first. You go first.

MAN: (*Also annoyed*) No, I offered first for you to go first, so you go first.

WOMAN: (*Annoyance building*) Well, I don't see why . . . (*Interrupted by whistle*)
            (*Three blasts of whistle cut in. On the first they freeze, and on the third they both turn and face JESUS*)

JESUS: As I was saying, I'm not forcing you to do anything, but . . . well, shall we give it one more try?
            (*JESUS blows whistle followed by the football clapping chant rhythm and a shout of 'Round Four'. A second whistle breaks freeze and MAN and WOMAN turn to each other*)

MAN/WOMAN: (*Together*) Darling, I'm sorry . . .

MAN: Oh, you go first.

WOMAN: Well . . . I'm sorry about your World Cup* wall-chart. I really didn't know that filling it in would upset you so much.

MAN: I know you didn't, pooch, it was just me being all silly and tetchy. I have a bad day at work and then always seem to take it out on you. I'm sorry.

---

* Replace as appropriate.

WOMAN: Well, anyway, from now on, I'll leave you to fill it in. OK?

MAN: Thanks. And about the . . . you know . . .

WOMAN: The toilet.

MAN: Yeah, look, I'm sorry. I'll have a word with the lads next time I see them. Hey, and I thought I might buy one of them signs you hang up over the toilet that says, 'If you sprinkle when you tinkle, be a sweet and wipe the seat.'

WOMAN: Well, it was more the sprinkles over the pipes and walls I was worried about, but thank you, darling, that sounds like a wonderful idea.

MAN: It's nice being nice to each other, isn't it?

WOMAN: Yeah, really nice. How about we have a quiet night in? Just us two, a bottle of wine and a romantic video.

MAN: Sounds good, but how about a good juicy thriller?

WOMAN: Oh no, not one of your bloodbaths. Let's just have a nice, gentle, romantic comedy.

MAN: Blluuurrgghhh! They are so sickly, love! Come on, let's agree on a good thriller.

WOMAN: (*Annoyance begins to build*) No, I want a romance.

MAN: Well, I want a thriller.

WOMAN: Romance.

MAN: Thriller.

WOMAN: (*Shouts*) Romance!

MAN: (*Shouts*) Thriller!
(*Builds up until we hear three long blasts on the whistle. Freeze and blackout*)

TEACHING POINT

Use your words to build people up rather than knock them down.

BIBLE REFERENCE

James 3:3–12

Ginger Snaps and Fondant Fancies

INTRODUCTION

If I were to ask you how relaxed a new person would feel at your church, what would your response be? Often we fall into our comfortable little cliques and make it incredibly hard for a newcomer to feel accepted. Jesus teaches us the importance of treating strangers well and making them feel welcome. In this sketch, set during the traditional post-service refreshments, Jesus himself tries unsuccessfully to break into an established clique.

Characters: MABEL; JOAN; JESUS.

MABEL and JOAN are standing centre stage, both holding a cup of tea and biscuit. JESUS is standing a few feet away, holding a cup. Occasionally they exchange glances.

MABEL: (*Bites biscuit*) Ooh, the ginger snaps aren't too good today, are they, Joan?

JOAN: Bit on the soggy side, Mabel.

MABEL: Who's on biscuit rota this week?

JOAN: Mary.

MABEL: Oh, say no more. That explains it. They'll be the cheap Tesco no-frills ones. When it's my turn on the rota, I always make a point of buying McVities'.

JOAN: Well, it's worth the few extra pence, isn't it?

MABEL: Course it is, Joan. As my mother always taught me, you get what you pay for. And I'm sorry to say it, but Mary always has been a bit of a cheap-skate.

JOAN: Mmmm . . . (*Pause*) Service was good today, wasn't it?

MABEL: Lovely. Father Humphrey has such a lovely way about him.

JOAN: Can't remember what it was about.

MABEL: No, me neither, but I don't necessarily think that matters.

JOAN: (*Quietly, indicating JESUS*) Did you see the new fella?

MABEL: Yes. What do you think he's up to?

JOAN: No idea. Be careful, he's right behind you. (*Both glance and smile. JESUS walks towards them*)

MABEL: Oh, my giddy aunt, he's coming over. What on earth can he want?

JESUS: Hello, ladies. How are you?

MABEL: (*Uncomfortably*) Fine, absolutely fine. Well, the ginger snaps are a bit on the soft side, but apart from that . . .

JESUS: Well, it's nice to meet you. My name is Jesus.

JOAN: I'm Joan, and this is my friend Mabel.

JESUS: Well, hello, Joan and Mabel. (*Uncomfortable silence*) So, have you been coming to this church long?

MABEL: (*Abruptly*) Yes we have! A goodly number of years.

JESUS: Ah, good. It's very nice here.

MABEL: I see you've got yourself a coffee. Didn't you get a ginger snap?

JESUS: Oh no, all the biscuits were gone, but it's not a problem.

MABEL: Oh yes, it is! That's that Harold. Honestly, he only comes to church for the flippin' biscuits, doesn't he, Joany? He really is the limit. Mary

should have kept some aside. She knows what
he's like. (*Shouts offstage to Mary*) Hey, Mary!
Are there any more ginger snaps left, or has
Harold the gannet scoffed the lot? (*To Jesus*) Yes,
go on, she says if you're sharpish, there's a few
left. Oh, and remember to put 15p in the dish for
next week's kitty. Just 'cos you're new you don't
get a freebie.

JESUS: Yeah, sure. (*JESUS exits*)

JOAN: Seems quite nice.

MABEL: Bit shifty if you ask me. And very rude butting in
          on our private conversation. What did he say his
          name was?

JOAN: I can't remember. Sounded familiar though.
          Sshhh, he's coming back. (*Shocked*) Oh look, I
          don't believe it!

MABEL: What? What is it?

JOAN: I think he's holding a . . . He has! He's got a
          fondant fancy!

MABEL: (*Annoyed*) A fondant fancy!

JESUS: (*Enters and rejoins MABEL and JOAN*) Hello,
          again. No more biscuits, but they did have a
          couple of cakes. (*MABEL and JOAN give him the
          silent treatment*) Are you OK?

MABEL: (*Stand-offish*) That looks very nice.

JESUS: Yes it is, thanks. Bit better than a soggy ginger
          snap.

MABEL: I hope you put your money in.

JESUS: Yes, I put a bit extra in as I got a cake.

MABEL: (*Irritated*) Yes, we know you got a cake. Don't
          rub it in. All the years I've served here, you'd
          think I'd get first refusal of the fondant fancies.
          Still, that's Mary Marshall for you!

JESUS: I'm sorry, would you like some?

MABEL: No, I wouldn't want to deprive you.

JESUS: (*Pause*) The vicar gave a good message today, didn't he?

MABEL: (*Bored, unresponsive*) Yeah.

JOAN: Yeah. (*Another uncomfortable silence*)

JESUS: Yes . . . well . . . Well, I'll leave you ladies to it then . . . I'll see you again sometime . . . or maybe not. (*JESUS exits*)

MABEL: Well, it's no surprise, is it?

JOAN: What isn't?

MABEL: It's no surprise when you get rude and pushy ones like him that we never get any new members.

JOAN: Oh, cheer up, Mabel. Let's go and see if there's any more fondant fancies left.

MABEL: All right. (*They begin to walk off*) Mary! (*Exit and blackout*)

TEACHING POINT

Always make newcomers at church feel really welcome.

BIBLE REFERENCES

Matthew 25:35, 40; Hebrews 13:2

Hypocritically Speaking

INTRODUCTION

This short piece looks at an aspect of 'modern-day Pharisaism' in the church. Jesus condemned in no uncertain terms the Pharisees' outward façade of righteousness, which masked all kinds of malice and self-interest. Although people's dismissal of Christianity on the grounds that 'the church is full of hypocrites' is ridiculous, we as Christians constantly need challenging to examine our thoughts, motives and attitudes.

Characters: JEAN; DENISE.

JEAN and DENISE enter from opposite sides of the stage. They speak to each other with false smiles and pleasantries. During the asides, they uncover their true feelings to the audience, while the other character holds a freeze.

JEAN: Oh, hello Denise. How lovely to see you again. (*Aside*) Ugghh, this woman is positively infuriating.

DENISE: You too, Jean. How long has it been? (*Aside*) Not long enough, I can tell you. I'd happily never lay eyes on her again in my life!

JEAN: Well, it must be a good few months.

DENISE: I'd say at least six. Did you help out at the church bazaar in March?

JEAN: Yes, I ran the tombola stall, made nearly two hundred and fifty pounds. (*Aside*) And I know for a fact her fair trade produce stall only made sixty-two pounds fifty!

DENISE: Oh, that was good. I did the fair trade stand. I can't remember how much I made though. (*Aside*) Huh, as if money's all that matters. Personally I think it's a lot more Christian to promote fair trading than unlicensed gambling!

JEAN: If you don't mind me saying, Denise, that is a lovely outfit. Is it Marks and Spencer's? (*Aside*) Have you ever seen anything quite so revolting in your life? I guarantee she got it for fifty pence at a car boot sale.

DENISE: No, it was Debenhams actually. Yours is very snazzy too. (*Aside*) Cheeky old moo! I wouldn't be seen dead in Marks and Sparks'. She, however, is the coiffured queen of Marks and Spencer's crimplene!

JEAN: Well, I try my best. Do you still do the teas and coffees at the Tuesday night prayer meeting? (*Aside*) The hypocrite will do anything to appear holy. Don't tell anybody I told you, but I've heard she fancies the cassock off Lionel, the new curate.

DENISE: Yes I do, funnily enough. I like to support Lionel as much as I can. (*Aside*) Not that she'd know anything about prayer meetings. The last time *she* prayed, Sean Connery* had a full head of hair!

JEAN: I must come along and have a proper catch-up with you one evening. That's the problem of going to such a large church, you can never keep up with anyone. (*Aside*) Thank heavens for small mercies. If I had to see dreary Denise every week, I think I'd turn from my faith.

---

* If you wish, Sean Connery can be substituted by a bald person present and known to the audience, as long as he has a good sense of humour!

DENISE: That would be lovely, Jean. You know my number, give us a ring any time. (*Aside*) Time to phone British Telecom to change my number.

JEAN: Well, you take care, Denise. I'll see you soon. (*Aside*) If I'm really unlucky.

DENISE: You too, Jean. Bye bye! (*Aside*) Dear God please protect us from hypocrites like her! (*As they exit to opposite sides, they wave and exchange sickly smiles. Fade to blackout*)

TEACHING POINT

Heart attitude is more important to God than outward appearance.

BIBLE REFERENCES

1 Samuel 16:7b; Matthew 23:25–28

Walter: The Insurance Policy

INTRODUCTION

My favourite round in the TV series *Whose Line Is It Anyway?* is called 'The world's worst . . .'. In these next two sketches, we are introduced to Walter, possibly the world's worst evangelist. Having grasped hold of Jesus' great commission in Matthew chapter 28, he takes things to an extreme – with hideous consequences.

The actor playing Walter must be able to build up a strong caricature to play the part, and also have an awareness of comic timing.

Characters: WALTER; MAN.

WALTER is doing some door-to-door evangelism using an 'interesting' approach. He enters and knocks on the MAN's door.

	(*MAN opens door*)
WALTER:	(*Confrontational*) Are you covered?
MAN:	Pardon?
WALTER:	Are you covered?
MAN:	I'm sorry. Whatever you're selling I'm really not interested.
WALTER:	(*Put out*) I'm not selling anything. I'm asking if you're covered.
MAN:	I really don't understand what you're talking about. Is it some kind of insurance policy you're offering?

WALTER: It's the only worthwhile insurance policy in existence, my friend.

MAN: Ah well, that's what they all say. What kind of a policy is it then? Home contents?

WALTER: No.

MAN: Car?

WALTER: No.

MAN: Life?

WALTER: Precisely!

MAN: Well, I'm sorry, but I've got a life insurance policy.

WALTER: Yes, but are you fully covered?

MAN: Well, I think it's pretty extensive. What exactly do you mean by fully covered?

WALTER: What I mean is, are you fully covered in the sacrificial blood of the Lamb?

MAN: (*Annoyed*) I *beg* your pardon? I'm a vegetarian!

WALTER: Are you rejecting me?

MAN: Well, I don't fancy being covered in oodles of lamb's blood, if that's what you mean!

WALTER: Because the Lord says, 'He who rejects you, rejects me; but he who rejects me, rejects him who sent me.'

MAN: What are you going on about now?

WALTER: I'm giving you the opportunity to take up your cross, to lay down your iniquities on the altar, and allow yourself to be soaked in the purifying qualities of the sacrificial blood of the Lamb. How can you reject that gift?

MAN: Sorry, mate, but I think you're a complete nutter!

WALTER: I warn you. In Matthew's Gospel we read, 'If anyone will not welcome you, or listen to your words, shake the dust off your feet when you leave that home.' I'm warning you, if you spurn me again, I will be forced to shake the dust from your path off my feet! (*He vigorously shakes his foot as he speaks*)

MAN: Well, have a nice shake. Goodbye. (*MAN exits*)

WALTER: (*Pause, then shakes his foot again*) Lord, once again I've been persecuted for the sake of your name. But your word says, 'Blessed are those who are persecuted because of righteousness, for theirs is the kingdom of heaven.' Thank you for that promise, Lord. It keeps me strong in service. Now, who's next? (*Blackout*)

TEACHING POINT

The importance of communicating the gospel effectively.

BIBLE REFERENCES

Matthew 5:10, 10:14, 28:16–20; Luke 10:16

Walter: The Blood Donor

INTRODUCTION

Walter is on the evangelism path again, this time in the hospital waiting room before donating blood. And yes, for those of you who remember, there are echoes of the late, great Tony Hancock!

Characters: WALTER; MAN.

MAN is sitting in waiting room looking worried. WALTER enters confidently. He sits down and starts slapping his forearm to find a prominent vein.

MAN: Is this your first time?
WALTER: Fifty-ninth.
MAN: Oh, quite an old hand then.
WALTER: Well, I like to do my bit when I can.
MAN: Very commendable I must say, very commendable. Does it hurt?
WALTER: No, just a little prick.
MAN: Oh, good. I've got a low pain threshold, you see. Anything in the slightest bit gory and I start to come over all funny.
WALTER: Don't be such a namby-pamby! Our pain is of no consequence compared to that of the Suffering Servant.
MAN: Who?
WALTER: (*Graphically*) We feel a mere needle in our arm, but he succumbed to a crown of thorns pressed

	into his head, nails driven into his wrists and feet . . .
MAN:	Ooohh! Stop! I told you what I'm like. You'll have me keeling over in a minute.
WALTER:	Brother, you've come to sacrifice a mere pint of your blood on the altar of the National Health Service, but have you discovered him who sacrificed everything to pay for your disgusting and revolting transgressions?
MAN:	(*Worried*) What did you just say?
WALTER:	I said, he sacrificed everything to pay for your disgusting and revolting transgressions.
MAN:	Not that bit! What did you say before that?
WALTER:	What, about sacrificing a mere pint of blood?
MAN:	That's it! Are you being serious?
WALTER:	About what?
MAN:	Exactly how much blood will I have to give?
WALTER:	A pint.
MAN:	(*Horrified*) A pint! Good gracious, man, that's very nearly an armful!
WALTER:	Oh, off goes Mr Namby-Pamby again. Our Saviour was flogged to the point of death. The whip they used was studded with sharp rocks, so the flesh was ripped off his back in strips. The blood literally poured . . .
MAN:	(*Interrupts*) *Stop!* I think I'm going to faint. (*He begins to go dizzy*)
WALTER:	Have you been crucified with Christ, brother? Galatians 2 says, 'I have been crucified with Christ, and I no longer live, but Christ lives in me.' I'm giving you the opportunity to take up your cross, allow yourself to be soaked in the purifying qualities of the sacrificial blood of the Lamb. Brother . . . (*Urgently*) brother! (*MAN has obviously fainted*) That's right, brother, you

just take a quiet moment to reflect. I'll go and get the . . . nurse . . . (*Shouts*) Nurse! (*Fade to blackout*)

TEACHING POINT

The importance of communicating the gospel effectively.

BIBLE REFERENCES

Matthew 28:16–20; Galatians 2:20

Reaching Out

Sketches for Use in Evangelism

Who Am I?

INTRODUCTION

In a wonderful quote in his book, *Mere Christianity*, C.S. Lewis argues that Jesus has left us with only three alternatives as to his nature: either he is mad, evil or truly the Son of God. He never meant to leave us with an option that he was a great moral teacher who was a good man.

This sketch takes a look at Jesus' claim and challenges the audience to make their choice. It has been written without too many specific directions, to encourage groups to be creative and make it very much their own. It would be equally useful to work on for performance or as a learn-by-doing exercise.

Characters: NARRATOR; THREE ACTORS; JESUS.

Cast stand frozen across stage. After a short time, the NARRATOR makes three beats using any suitable instrument. You can use anything from a drum or dustbin lid to two wooden sticks.

NARRATOR: From the beginning of time, God had a plan.
ONE: A good plan.
TWO: A very good plan.
THREE: A very very good plan.
NARRATOR: To send his Son Jesus (*JESUS steps forward*) to live on planet earth and mix with all different kinds of human beings.

ONE: (*Posh*) Pleasure to meet you, Jesus.

TWO: (*Common*) All right, mate?

THREE: (*Nerdy*) Ooh, hello.

NARRATOR: He learnt his Father's trade as a carpenter and became a master craftsman. (*Short mime using all four actors illustrating carpentry. Short vocals may also be used*) On his thirtieth birthday (*ONE, TWO and THREE burst into a short and spontaneous rendition of 'Happy Birthday'*) he gave up his trade and became a full-time preacher. (*JESUS moves to centre stage and stands on a block holding a preaching pose. ONE, TWO and THREE gather around*) He spoke to thousands of people about living lives full of – love (*As each virtue is spoken, JESUS adopts a new preaching pose and ONE, TWO and THREE break into various poses with sound effects to demonstrate. These should be quick-fire and humorous*) joy – peace – patience – kindness – and self-control. (*At the end, ONE, TWO and THREE should be frozen facing upstage towards JESUS*) After he spoke, he would perform great miracles – healing the lame (*JESUS steps down and touches ONE on the head*)

ONE: (*Turns around*) I can walk!

NARRATOR: Curing the blind (*JESUS touches TWO on the head*)

TWO: (*Turns around*) I can see!

NARRATOR: And turning gallons of water into wine. (*JESUS touches THREE on the head*)

THREE: (*Turns around stumbling*) Cheers, Jesus! (*Hiccups*)

NARRATOR: Everybody agreed that he was definitely . . .

ONE: A nice man.

TWO: A very nice man.

THREE: A very very nice man.

NARRATOR: But after hearing him speak and seeing him perform great miracles, the people all wanted to know exactly who he was.

ONE: (*Turning to TWO*) Who is he?

TWO: I don't know. (*Turns to THREE*) Who is he?

THREE: I don't know. (*Turns to JESUS*) Who are you?

JESUS: (*Short pause*) I am the Son of God. (*Three loud beats by the NARRATOR*)

NARRATOR: His claim to be the Son of God sent fear through the government and corrupt religious leaders, so they secretly plotted the murder of Jesus, accusing him of –

ONE: Blasphemy. (*As these are spoken, ONE, TWO and THREE face audience in stillness*)

TWO: Heresy.

THREE: Treason.

ONE: Blasphemy.

TWO: Heresy.

THREE: Treason.

NARRATOR: Jesus was turned over to face trumped-up charges of blasphemy and high treason. But the authorities were too late. (*As this is being spoken, JESUS slowly walks to the rear centre of stage*) The effect Jesus had had on the people was phenomenal. By his life and claims, he had left the people with three alternatives. Either he was stark raving mad (*ONE, TWO and THREE adopt 'mad' pose*), a liar and a fraud who was maliciously evil (*ONE, TWO and THREE adopt evil pose*), or he was, as he had claimed, the

Son of God. (*ONE, TWO and THREE turn to JESUS*)

The religious leaders using threats (*ONE, TWO and THREE pose threateningly*) and bribes (*ONE, TWO and THREE mime bribes*) persuaded the crowd to turn against Jesus, and when they had the chance to let him go free, they all rallied against him and cried out . . .

ONE: (*Turns and shouts*) Crucify him! (*As he shouts, NARRATOR does a beat and JESUS who is centre stage throws up his right arm to form first part of cross*)

TWO: (*Turns and shouts*) Crucify him! (*As he shouts, NARRATOR does a second beat and JESUS throws up his left arm to form second part of the cross*)

THREE: (*Turns and shouts*) Crucify him! (*As he shouts, NARRATOR does a third beat and JESUS drops his head. Either ONE, TWO or THREE now vocalises the sound of JESUS' heartbeat slowing down. This should continue through the next sequence*)

NARRATOR: As Jesus died on the cross, the last thing he saw was the crowd spitting (*ONE, TWO and THREE in turn 'spit' towards JESUS*) and jeering. (*ONE, TWO and THREE join together to make jeering noise. The sound of JESUS' heartbeat now slows down to a stop*) Even in death Jesus challenged the crowds with the question, Who do you say I am? Am I stark raving mad, am I a cruel and evil liar, or am I truly the Son of God? Two thousand years on, the question remains the same.

*(The freeze is held with JESUS on the cross
and ONE, TWO and THREE looking
towards him. Out of the silence we hear quiet
singing by one of the cast. A loud final beat is
followed by blackout)*

TEACHING POINT

Jesus challenges us today, just as he did two thousand years
ago, to decide who he is.

BIBLE REFERENCE

John 19:1–30

Calendar System

INTRODUCTION

In this sketch, two friends debate the existence and relevance of Jesus. Kate introduces an interesting argument that the calendar system revolves around Jesus' life on earth – strong evidence for his significance on the world stage.

Characters: BRIAN; KATE. (The sketch has been written for a man and a woman but could easily be adapted.)

KATE is seated centre stage reading the Bible. BRIAN enters.

BRIAN: Oh no, do me a favour. You're not reading that Bible again.

KATE: (*Looks at cover*) Apparently so . . . .

BRIAN: I really don't know why you bother. You might just as well read a copy of *Aesop's Fables* for all the truth you're gonna find in there.

KATE: (*Sarcastically*) Oh, excuse me, Mr Theological Giant.

BRIAN: Look, I don't claim to have read it, but come on. Jesus Christ, Son of God – it's pathetic. Even if he did exist as some kind of bearded, sandalled nomad two thousand years ago, that doesn't affect us today.

KATE: You really believe that Jesus Christ has no relevance at all?

BRIAN: Not a jot.

KATE: Have you got your diary on you?

BRIAN: (*Looks confused*) My diary? Yeah, course. (*Gets it out of his pocket and hands it to KATE*)

KATE: (*Points*) What does that say?

BRIAN: Ooh yeah, lunch at 12.30 with Sandra from the newsagent's.

KATE: No! Not that. There! (*Points again*)

BRIAN: What? The date? June 1999.*

KATE: (*In deep thought*) Nineteen hundred and ninety-nine.* World's young, isn't it?

BRIAN: Well, it's been going for a bit longer than that.

KATE: How much longer?

BRIAN: I don't know. What is this? A history lesson? Must be a few hundred thousand years, probably more.

KATE: Well, why does the date only say 1999* then?

BRIAN: That's obviously when they started the calendar system, isn't it?

KATE: So, how can we date something that happened more than 2,000 years ago?

BRIAN: Are you totally deranged? Dates are now carried forward with the letters AD in front of them, and anything earlier is counted in reverse followed by the letters BC. Didn't they teach you anything at school?

KATE: All right, clever clogs, what do BC and AD stand for then?

BRIAN: Before Christ and . . . (*Tails off, realising he's been caught out*)

KATE: (*Sarcastically*) Pardon? I didn't catch that. Did you say 'before Christ'? Let me get this straight. You think the world's calendar system is centred around a totally irrelevant man, who possibly didn't exist. Seems a bit unlikely, doesn't it?

---

* Replace with current date.

(*KATE is now really having fun at BRIAN's expense*) I mean, you think they would have found someone a bit better to bestow this honour on . . . Julius Caesar, Cleopatra, the Spice Girls* . . . Hey, that's not a bad idea. Maybe we can start a new calendar system around them. (*BRIAN slowly exits*) Before the formation of the Spice Girls,* BSG.* After the demise of the Spice Girls,* ADSG.* What do you think of that, Brian, eh? Brian . . . (*Blackout*)

TEACHING POINT

Jesus Christ is *the* pivotal figure in human history.

BIBLE REFERENCES

John 1:1; Hebrews 13:8

---

* Replace with more topical reference as necessary.

Millennium Party

INTRODUCTION

At the centre of this sketch are three lads who are at a celebration – but they don't know why! Joining in with a party
when we don't know why or who it's for seems utterly ridiculous. But millions will be doing this during the millennium
celebrations. This sketch, accompanied by a short talk communicating the relevance of the millennium, will have a powerful impact in any setting, particularly evangelistic. It
obviously has a shorter 'shelf-life' than the other sketches in
this book, but it could be safely used to good effect throughout the year 2000.

Characters: GAZ; BAZ; DAZ; DAVE.

*Loud music and cheering is heard offstage. As it fades, GAZ,
BAZ and DAZ enter in a chain, doing the conga.*

GAZ/BAZ/DAZ:	(*Singing*) Oooh ooh ooh, come on and do the conga, ooh it's conga night for sure. (*They break from the chain, short pause before bursting into the opening of 'Agadoo'*) Agadoo doo doo, push pine-apple shake a tree . . .
GAZ:	(*Stops them*) Enough of that, boys. Let's see if there's any lager! (*All cheer*) Here Baz, chuck us a Fosters.
BAZ:	(*Dodgy Australian accent*) No problem mate, can of fozzies coming up! (*Throws*

206

	GAZ a can) How about you, Bruce? Do you wanna tinny?
DAZ:	My name ain't Bruce. It's Daz, you pillock.
BAZ:	(*Continues Australian accent*) I know that, you daft sheila! Now do you want some of the old amber nectar or not?
DAZ:	(*Annoyed*) Did you call me Sheila? Are you casting dispersions?
BAZ:	(*Back to normal voice*) Oh shut up dopey, drink up. (*Throws DAZ a can*)
DAZ:	That's more like it. Cheers, boys!
GAZ/BAZ/DAZ:	(*Together*) Cheers!
GAZ:	And to go with the Fosters dry white 1998, who fancies a handful of scrumptious Pringles? (*He produces a tube of Pringles*)
BAZ:	Oh, I dunno about that mate, 'cos once you pop . . .
GAZ/BAZ/DAZ:	(*Together*) You can't stop! (*They all start rhythmically slapping thighs, chest, cheeks, etc., as in advert*)
DAZ:	Over 'ere, Gaz.
GAZ:	Okay, Daz. (*Passes Pringles*) Baz?
BAZ:	Yeah, Gaz.
GAZ:	There you go, Baz. (*Passes Pringles*)
BAZ:	Cheers, Gaz.
	(*Short pause as they all scrunch loudly, making grunts of satisfaction*)
GAZ:	I didn't fancy yours much, Baz.
BAZ:	(*Defensive*) What are you on about, Gaz?
GAZ:	I saw you chatting that bird up, the one whose skirt was slightly longer than my belt.
BAZ:	I weren't chatting her up. I used to go to

	school with her, that's all. What about you then, squirming round that old trollop, with her make-up about six inches thick!
GAZ:	Do you mind? That was my sister.
DAZ:	No it wasn't Gaz, I was chatting your sister up in the kitchen all night.
GAZ/BAZ:	(*Together*) Ugghhhh!
GAZ:	Any luck with her then?
DAZ:	No! I think there must be something wrong with her eyesight. She said she didn't fancy me.
GAZ:	Well, I'll give her a bit of credit for intelligence then. (*GAZ and BAZ both laugh*)
DAZ:	(*Sarcastic*) Oh ha ha, you two are well funny, aren't you?
DAVE:	(*Enters*) Hello guys, how are you doing?
GAZ:	Brill.
BAZ:	Great thanks mate.
DAZ:	All right, except for Morecambe and Wise here.
DAVE:	Enjoying the party then?
GAZ:	Yeah, it's pukka mate, pukka. Do you wanna tin of Fosters?
DAVE:	Yeah, cheers.
GAZ:	(*Passes a can*) Pringles? (*Offers some*)
DAVE:	Ta. Can I ask you a question?
BAZ:	Course you can pal, fire away.
DAVE:	Well, do you know what this party's in aid of exactly?
BAZ:	Er . . . no! Do you know, Gaz? Daz? (*Both shake heads in confusion*)
DAVE:	Is it for a birthday, wedding, anniversary?
GAZ:	No idea, mate.

DAVE:	Well, if you don't know what it's for, you must at least know *who* it's for.
DAZ:	No, sorry pal. Can't help you out on that front either.
DAVE:	In that case, excuse me for asking and all that, but why are you at a party when you don't know who or what it's for?
GAZ:	Well, that's easy, innit? Lager!
BAZ:	Women!
DAZ:	Music!
GAZ:	Pringles!
BAZ:	And not forgetting, Twiglets! (*Shoves two twiglets up his nostrils, GAZ and DAZ laugh hysterically*) You are now entering the Twiglet zone.
GAZ:	Come on mate, lighten up, it's a party. You should be enjoying yourself! Let's get back in there, boys, we've deprived all them girls long enough. (*They all cheer*) All follow me! (*They get in a chain, and exit performing the conga again*)
DAVE:	(*Pauses in amazement, smiles and raises his tin*) Happy millennium! (*Fade to blackout*)

TEACHING POINT

Without Jesus Christ, there wouldn't be a millennium, let alone any celebrations.

BIBLE REFERENCE

Matthew 16:13–17

The Doctor's Dilemma

INTRODUCTION

Jesus teaches us that he came to earth for the sake of the sinners, not the righteous – in the same way that a doctor cares for sick people, not healthy ones. The point being made in this sketch is that people often refuse to admit there is anything wrong, so miss out on the help available to them if they would simply ask.

The doctor in this piece is, in effect, Jesus, and the patient represents anyone who stubbornly refuses to turn to Christ for help, even though they are in desperate need.

Characters: DOCTOR; ERNEST MORIBUND, the patient.

DOCTOR sits at his desk scribbling notes. ERNEST is sitting in the waiting room in obvious discomfort, smoking, drinking, coughing and making noises of excruciating pain.

DOCTOR: Next patient, please.
ERNEST: Oh, that must be me. (*Struggles to get up, in great pain*) Ooh, flippin' 'eck! Blimey O'Riley! (*When he finally struggles up, his leg won't work*)
DOCTOR: Next patient, please!
ERNEST: (*Coughing loudly*) With you in a second, doc. (*Starts punching his leg*) Come on, wake up, you bloomin' stupid thing. (*Leg starts to move*) Aha, we're off. (*Enters surgery*) Good morning, doctor.

DOCTOR: Ah, good morning. Mr Moribund, isn't it?

ERNEST: That's right, doc. Ernest J. Moribund, sixty-one years old, and in the prime of health.

DOCTOR: Yes, well, would you like to take a seat?

ERNEST: Thanks, doc. (*Moves to seat and very slowly, with painful grimaces, lowers himself into the chair*)

DOCTOR: Have you got a problem with your back, Mr Moribund?

ERNEST: (*Defensively*) My back! No, solid as a rock that is. A hundred press-ups and fifty squat thrusts a day, that back does.

DOCTOR: Well, if you say so, Mr Moribund. Now, we just need to do an annual check-up for you today. Are there any health-related issues I can help you with?

ERNEST: No, doc. In tip-top condition I am. Well, considering I'm sixty-one, I'm not bad anyway.

DOCTOR: (*Puts stethoscope to ERNEST's chest*) Mr Moribund, can I ask if you smoke at all?

ERNEST: (*Still smoking and holding a bottle of booze from the waiting room*) Me? Smoke? No, absolutely disgusting habit if you ask me, doc. And if you don't mind me saying, a total waste of money. I prefer to spend my money on a wide selection of healthy vitamin pills.

DOCTOR: What about alcohol?

ERNEST: Well, if you're offering . . .

DOCTOR: No, Mr Moribund, I was asking how much alcohol you consume.

ERNEST: Oh, I see. Teetotal me, never touch the stuff. No, I tell a lie. I did push myself to half a glass of Babycham at my daughter's wedding ten years ago, but apart from that . . .

DOCTOR: Regular exercise?

ERNEST: (*Pause to think*) Well, that's tricky. You see, I don't so much see it as regular exercise as such. My lifestyle is really just one long keep-fit regime.

DOCTOR: Well, Mr Moribund, I must say what I'm hearing all sounds very commendable, but are you really sure there's nothing I can do to help you in any way? All you need to do is ask, and I'm sure I'd have some advice or medication to cure just about anything.

ERNEST: Well, I hate to let you off so lightly, doc, but I simply can't think of a single thing.

DOCTOR: In that case, I think your check-up's over. Thanks for coming in, and if there's anything I can help you with at any time, please don't hesitate to contact me. (*DOCTOR signs paper and hands it to ERNEST*)

ERNEST: (*Slowly gets back up*) Ta very much, doc. (*Exits surgery*) Look at that, a clean bill of health. The Missus won't believe it!

TEACHING POINT

Only when we confess our sin and repent can Jesus cure us of our terminal spiritual illness.

BIBLE REFERENCE

Mark 2:17

The Titch and the Tree

INTRODUCTION

This slant on the ever-popular story of Zacchaeus involves the reaction of a talking tree. Imagination will be required to transform the actor into a tree, using costume and props plus, if possible, a stepladder. The actor playing Zacchaeus should walk on his knees with shoes attached. For the majority of the sketch he will be up the tree, so it won't cause a huge problem.

Characters: ZACCHAEUS; TREE

TREE is positioned centre stage. ZACCHAEUS enters, walking on his knees. He is apparently struggling to see something in the distance. In his frustration, he spots TREE and makes his way over. ZACCHAEUS then begins to climb.

TREE: Ow!

ZACCH: Who was that?

TREE: Me!

ZACCH: Who's me?

TREE: Me, you big lumbering oaf! (*ZACCHAEUS still can't see*) Down here (*ZACCHAEUS finally sees TREE*)

ZACCH: (*Shocked*) You're a tree!

TREE: (*Sarcastic*) Ooh, make way for Albert Einstein.

ZACCH: But trees can't speak.

TREE: Well, mate, either I'm speaking or you've

completely lost your marbles. (*Short pause as ZACCHAEUS fidgets*) Owww!!

ZACCH: Oh, sorry, did I kick you in the spine?

TREE: (*Annoyed*) Of course you didn't kick me in the spine, you berk! I'm a tree. I haven't got a spine. You just knocked a bit of bark off my nether regions!

ZACCH: I'm really sorry.

TREE: Well, what are you doing clambering all over me anyway? As if I don't have enough problems with snotty-nosed little brats swinging all over me, giving me lumbago.

ZACCH: I'm just trying to get a better view of Jesus.

TREE: Well, why don't you go over there with everybody else?

ZACCH: I would but . . . well, I'm what you might call vertically challenged.

TREE: (*Sarcastic*) Vertically challenged! What's that, the politically correct way of saying you're a titch?

ZACCH: I suppose so, yeah.

TREE: Don't try and pull the wool over my eyes, mate. I'm not daft. My roots are firmly planted in the earth. What's your name, then?

ZACCH: Zacchaeus. And yours?

TREE: Sycamore. Nice to meet you. (*Awkward moment as they try and figure out how to shake hands. Eventually ZACCHAEUS shakes a branch*) Hang on a minute, what did you say your name was?

ZACCH: Zacchaeus.

TREE: Blimey, that rings a bell. Now where have I heard that name before? Oh, it's gonna annoy me now. Ooh, I remember. Yes, there were two old girls leaning against me the other day, having a fag and a gossip. They were laying into this guy called Zacchaeus good and proper. (*Adopts moany woman voice*) 'Oh, that Zacchaeus is a crooked, ugly warthog, overcharging people on their taxes, having them thrown out of their houses. Honestly, he's a big scum-sucking pimple on the bottom of humanity.' (*Reverts to normal voice*) I tell you, he was not a popular chap at all.

ZACCH: That's me.

TREE: What?

ZACCH: I'm the very same crooked, ugly warthog they were talking about.

TREE: Uggghhh! Well, I hope it's not catching. I'll probably end up with Dutch elm disease cavorting with the likes of you!

ZACCH: That's why I need to see Jesus. I want to change my ways.

TREE: Don't take it personally, pal, but he's a busy man, and I'm sure he's got higher priorities than you.

ZACCH: But if I could just speak with him, I'm sure I could become a new man.

TREE: Well, I wouldn't hold your breath, mate. There's the best part of a thousand people over there, all wanting a tête-à-tête with the preacher man, so I don't much rate your chances. (*Short pause then look of shock*) Here, wait a minute . . .

ZACCH: What?

TREE: He's looking over here! (*ZACCHAEUS looks up, then joins TREE in look of stunned shock*) He's looking right at you!

ZACCH: Blimey, he's coming over. What do I say?

TREE: Don't ask me, I'm only a tree!

ZACCH: I know! I'll invite him to come to my house for a cup of tea.

TREE: Tsshh! Pathetic! That'll never work. (*They both continue to stare into distance as lights fade to blackout*)

TEACHING POINT

Jesus loves us all unconditionally.

BIBLE REFERENCE

Luke 19:1–10

Filthy Rags

INTRODUCTION

I originally wrote this piece as a sketch for four people, but over the years it has developed into a monologue, in which form I believe it is most powerful. The actor must communicate the man's fast-disappearing confidence in his own achievements, as he gives an account of his life. It can be used in a number of settings, but assuming the audience have no prior knowledge of the Scriptures, it may need to be supported by some form of talk.

Characters: PETER (plus offstage VOICE).

As lights go up, we see PETER sitting on a chair centre stage. On his lap is a briefcase which he is staring at. A bell is rung and we hear the offstage VOICE.

VOICE: Number 34863214, Mr Peter Benevolence. Time to give your account please.

PETER: (*He looks up and slowly steps forward. When he speaks it is in a confident manner*) Ah, hello. Do you mind if I . . . ? (*Indicates putting briefcase down, which he does*) Thank you. So this is where I find out if I take the up or down escalator! (*No response*) Well, I understand it's an account you want. It's difficult to know where to start really. As in all good films, maybe I'll start at the end, and do the whole thing in flashback.

217

You know, it's amazing how you always wonder and worry about suffering some horrific death in a spectacular accident or from some life-draining disease, but nothing could ever have prepared me for my untimely demise. Picture the scene. I'm walking to work, a delicious packed lunch of spam sandwiches in the briefcase, minding my own business, and all of a sudden (*Claps*) a chimney-pot falls on my head! Ooh, what a terrible mess, blood and gore all over the shop, and the next thing I know, here I am. Totally unbelievable, isn't it? You probably don't believe me. (*Slaps head*) What am I talking about, you don't believe me. Of course you believe me. I suppose you knew it all anyway. Yes . . .

Anyway, back to my account. I had planned ahead, in anticipation of a scenario such as this, so I've got everything possibly relevant recorded, logged and filed in my briefcase. For starters, I've been a regular church-goer all my life, every Christmas, every Easter and a mass of weddings, funerals, christenings, etcetera, etcetera, and on each occasion I made a very generous donation to the church funds, of the rustling not rattling kind, if you get my drift. Anyway, all this has been receipted and logged in the little black cash book. I also have records of my long and prolific history of generous and regular giving to charity. I'll just name a few of the beneficiaries – RNLI, RSPCA, RSPB, NCH, NSPCC, ACET, ABC, XYZ and the BFG. (*Looks confused*) Or is that a book? Anyway, all records are in the trusty briefcase, and can be found logged in the dark green accounts book. What else shall I tell you about? Ooh yes, good deeds. How could I forget? Money doesn't solve everything. Well, to be honest, I've done it all – from the charity jumble sales and helping old dears across the street, to making myself available for doing odd jobs for old folks, or old jobs for odd folks as I used to humorously call it. (*Laughs to himself which soon tails off*) Yes, I always used to put real money and not bits of cut-up newspaper in the Christian Aid envelopes, and I even went to see a gospel concert by Sir Cliff Richard, just the once, ticket-stub retained. All this information, and more, in the navy blue file entitled 'Good Works'.

Well, how am I doing? I think I've got everything covered. What more can I say? I've been a nice guy, good to my family and friends. On the religious side of things, I suppose I've never been the fanatical type, but I don't necessarily see that as a bad thing, do you? I mean, just think of the number of wars that have kicked off in the name of religion. Not to say that's your fault, of course. No. You see, my faith has always been a very personal thing, just between me and . . . well, me and me, I suppose. I've always believed in you, well, sort of, ish, although I must admit it's quite overwhelming to actually meet you like this. (*Short pause then shouts, agitated*) Say something! Aren't you going to say anything? It's not going too well, is it? What else can I say? Look in the case, for God's . . . (*Stops himself, calms down*) Please just look in the case. (*He picks up case. As he opens it, a pile of filthy rags falls out. He freezes. We hear some quiet music, then the offstage VOICE speaks over it*)

VOICE: All of us have become like one who is unclean, and all our righteous acts are like filthy rags. We all shrivel up like a leaf, and like the wind our sins sweep us away.

PETER: (*Quietly*) Father, don't you remember me?

VOICE: I never knew you. Away from me. (*Music stops and PETER breaks from freeze*)

PETER: So, which escalator do I take? Up or . . . up or down? (*Pause*) Thank you. (*He picks up case, takes a deep breath and exits meaningfully. Blackout*)

TEACHING POINT

Good deeds and a 'religious' appearance are no substitute for a personal relationship with Jesus.

BIBLE REFERENCES

Isaiah 64:6; Matthew 7:21–23; Ephesians 2:8, 9

Route Planner

INTRODUCTION

This short piece illustrates Jesus' famous words in John chapter 14: 'I am the way, the truth and the life.' The Bible clearly sets out the route to God the Father through his Son, yet so many people are floundering around, trying to find the way.

The action takes place in a car with a married couple debating the best route. The piece is suitable for any audience.

Characters: ALAN; TINA.

Music is playing as lights come up, preferably a song about cars or driving. ALAN and TINA are in the front seats of a car. As the music stops the car screeches to a halt. ALAN starts looking at the map, TINA looks on frustrated.

TINA: So, we're lost, are we? Again!

ALAN: (*Defensively*) No! I'm just temporarily unsure of exactly where we are.

TINA: (*Unconvinced*) Mmm, lost!

ALAN: (*Looking at map in confusion*) Loopervil? Where's that then?

TINA: *Liverpool*! You've got the map upside down, you prize prune! (*TINA turns map around*)

ALAN: (*Embarrassed*) Yeah, I know. I was just trying to look at the roads from a different angle.

TINA: I don't know, you and your flippin' short-cuts.

ALAN: There's nothing wrong with my short-cuts!

TINA: Oh no! Name me one that's actually worked.

ALAN: Er . . . Ah! What about my cunningly clever route from Manchester to York?

TINA: Yeah, via Cardiff! Very cunning. And remember the time you offered to take me on a romantic trip to London for the royal wedding?

ALAN: What about it?

TINA: By the time we got there, they were getting a divorce!

ALAN: Well, that's hardly my fault, is it? (*Pause*) While we've stopped, you might as well chuck us a sarnie.

TINA: (*Picks up Tupperware*) Paste or sandwich spread?

ALAN: What flavour paste?

TINA: Beef.

ALAN: Oh great, she's trying to give me BSE now!

TINA: Well, have the sandwich spread then!

ALAN: No, I'll risk it. (*Starts eating sandwich*)

TINA: So, having deliberated over the map and our current predicament, have you got *any* idea yet of whereabouts in this fair land we actually are?

ALAN: (*Chomping on sandwich*) Well, love, it's not quite as easy to answer as all that.

TINA: Yes or no?

ALAN: No!

TINA: Great! Why can't you just follow the map? We have our own copy of *The Road User's Bible*, and I even phoned the AA to give me a plan of the optimum route. But no, in your wisdom, you felt it was better to aimlessly blunder around, hoping we might stumble on a better solution.

ALAN: Well, there might be another better way to get there.

TINA: There is no other way! The map is the way, the truth and the life. No man will come to Scarborough but by me.

ALAN: (*Pause*) That sounds familiar.

TINA: Yeah, I heard it somewhere. Can't remember where. Anyway, are you going to get onto the right road and follow the map, or are we going to flounder around for all time and eternity?

ALAN: (*Looks at map*) Umm . . . Ahh . . .

TINA: (*Impatiently*) Well? (*Lights fade to blackout*)

TEACHING POINT

The only way to a relationship with God the Father is via the route provided through Jesus Christ.

BIBLE REFERENCE

John 14:6

Starry-Eyed Bloggs

INTRODUCTION

The Bloggs family sit around musing over the newspapers and television. Miss Bloggs is reading her stars and the conversation turns to the reliability of astrology. Strong caricature performances and lots of laughs should be the target in this piece.

Characters: MR BLOGGS; MRS BLOGGS; MASTER BLOGGS; MISS BLOGGS.

As lights go up, MRS, MISS and MASTER BLOGGS are reading. MR BLOGGS is looking bored.

MR: Miss Bloggs, are you finished with my newspaper yet?

MISS: No.

MRS: Huh! Newspaper? Is that what you call *The Sun*?

MR: Don't be cheeky, Mrs Bloggs.

MRS: Well, it's a load of rubbish, innit? All it's got is page after page of sport and half-clad women.

MR: I think that might be a slight exaggeration, Mrs Bloggs. There also happens to be lots of interesting articles on current affairs.

MRS: Yeah, like who Jim Davidson's having a current affair with maybe. I told you to get *The Daily Mail*, I like the *Mail*.

MR: Well, go and get *The Daily Mail* then! I like *The*

	Sun, when I get a chance to read it! Can I have it now, Miss Bloggs?
MISS:	In a minute. I've nearly finished.
MR:	Creeping ivy! You put it down for two minutes to fetch a drink, and whoosh, it's gone. (*MISS BLOGGS rips half a page out of newspaper*) Oi! What are you playing at?
MISS:	You can have it back now.
MR:	What's left of it!
MISS:	I've only ripped the stars out.
MR:	What about the other side?
MISS:	It's an advert for Peugeot 106.
MR:	Oh great! I was thinking of buying a Peugeot 106.
MRS:	Ha! What with? Your lottery winnings? (*MISS and MRS laugh*)
MR:	That was a bit below the belt, Mrs Bloggs. You know I've never won anything on the lottery.
MRS:	Well, shut yer cakehole about buying a Peugeot 106 then!
MR:	(*Turns to his son for moral support*) I don't know, Master Bloggs, it's obviously too much to expect people not to assassinate your newspaper in this house.
MRS:	Oh, shut up! Here look Miss Bloggs, there's a good article in my *Bella* about why powerful men are sexy.
MR:	Huh! You wanna skip them bits and take more notice of the *Bella* 'Top Ten Cooking Tips'. I'm sure burning the dinner every night isn't one of them!
MRS:	That ain't burnt, Mr Bloggs, it's char-grilled.
MR:	Char-grilled burgers I've heard of, char-grilled steaks I like, but char-grilled fish fingers – ?
MISS:	Ignore him, Mrs Bloggs.

MRS: I will, Miss Bloggs, don't you worry. (*Pause*) Ooh look, *Family Fortunes* is on.

MR: Oh, I love this. The families are so thick. We should go on it, you know. What do you think, Master Bloggs?

MASTER: Oh I don't know about that, Mr Bloggs.

MR: Mrs Bloggs's a bit of a whizz on the quiz shows, aren't you?

MRS: (*Modest*) Well . . .

MR: She got a four-letter word on *Countdown* last week, didn't you? What was it?

MRS: 'Frog'.

MR: Frog. Good, eh?

MRS: I can't do them maths ones though.

MR: Well, nobody can. I reckon they have a calculator to work it out behind their desks.

MASTER: Don't be daft!

MR: And that Carol Vaudeville. Widen the camera angle and I guarantee she's got a whacking great computer to work 'em all out!

MRS: He's a right wally and all . . . that Richard Whiteley. All them horrible ties and jackets he wears.

MR: Les-'Family-Fortunes'-Dennis ain't much better.

MISS: Forget *Family Fortunes*. Who wants me to do their real fortune? Mrs Bloggs?

MRS: Oh go on then, Miss Bloggs.

MISS: Right, Sagittarius innit? Ooh, it's a good one. 'Romantic liaisons are having a revival. If you're on the lookout, a passing flirtation could turn into a full-blown fling. So put on your party frock, and look enchanting. Make sure your window of opportunity doesn't pass you by.'

MRS: Ooh!

MR: Load of tosh!

MISS: Capricorn for Mr Bloggs.

MR: No, I'm not interested in all that rubbish. (*Mimics MISS BLOGGS*) 'Put on a party frock, a passing flirtation could turn into a full-blown fling.' (*Normal voice*) I should be so lucky! (*MRS BLOGGS digs his ribs*)

MISS: What about you, Master Bloggs?

MASTER: No, I'm with Mr Bloggs on this one. It's not really my thing.

MISS: (*Sarcastic*) I suppose it's all anti your Bible, is it?

MASTER: Well, the Bible does actually warn against astrology, yes. Anyway, according to you, as I'm a Taurus, I should be hot-tempered, and I'm not, am I?

MISS: Ah, that's 'cos you were born in the cusp of Gemini.

MR: Cusp of Gemini? What a load of twaddle!

MASTER: Sorry, Miss Bloggs, but it just doesn't wash with me.

MISS: Oh, you're so gullible – and brainwashed by what the Bible says.

MASTER: OK, I admit I put my trust in what the Bible says, but the Dead Sea Scrolls and lots of other evidence point conclusively to its authenticity. I'm putting my faith on a safe bet. What I don't understand, Miss Bloggs, is how you seem so willing to put all your faith in Mystic Meg and Russell Grant! Who's the gullible and brainwashed one now?

MR: (*Laughs*) Nice one, Master Bloggs. Admit it, Miss Bloggs, he's got you there.

MISS: (*Annoyed*) Oh, get lost Mr Bloggs, I'm watching *Family Fortunes*.

MR: Ooh, temper temper! (*MRS BLOGGS starts to*

exit) Where are you going, Mrs Bloggs? Off to get your *Mail*?

MRS: In a manner of speaking, yes, you could say that. I just thought I'd go and put my party frock on ready for that fling. (*MR BLOGGS looks worried, then realises she's joking. They all begin to laugh. Fade to blackout*)

TEACHING POINT

The Bible is the only reliable source of guidance for life.

BIBLE REFERENCE

Isaiah 47:13–15

Christmas Is Coming

Sketches with a Christmas Theme

The Registrar

INTRODUCTION

This sketch brings the events of the Christmas story into the present time, and sees Joseph battling with bureaucracy as he tries to register the birth of Jesus. It can be used in any Christmas context as a funny and alternative view of the most famous birth in history.

Characters: BERNICE and LINDA, brash chatterboxes who work at the Registry Office; JOSEPH, long-suffering, and earthly father of Jesus.

There are two desks at either end of the stage. BERNICE and LINDA sit behind one chatting. The other desk has a chair on either side of it. There is also a line of chairs all along the rear of the stage.

BERNICE: No! You 'aven't got a clue wot you're talking about, Lind. His hair's absolutely disgusting! (*JOSEPH enters*)

LINDA: Disgusting! Oh, how can you say that? It's bee-aauutiful. All sexy and spiky. At least it don't flop all over his face.

JOSEPH: Excuse me please. (*Totally ignored*)

LINDA: Style! Oh, come of it Bernice, he has it covering his face 'cos he's so ugly.

BERNICE: *Ugly!* Oh, that is a joke, innit! I'll have you know he's just won the *Smash Hits'* Most

Gorgeous Guy in the Universe poll, and where was old spiky in that, eh?

JOSEPH: Excuse me please, I'd like to register a birth.

BERNICE: (*Tutting and irritated*) Have you got a ticket?

JOSEPH: A ticket?

BERNICE: Yes sir, a ticket. (*Turns to Linda*) Sorry for this gentleman's rude interruption, Linda. I'll continue our discussion in a moment. (*Turns back to JOSEPH and speaks to him in patronising tones*) If you get a ticket from that little machine on the wall, it has on it a number. When I call the number that is on your ticket, it's your turn to be served. Thank you. (*Turns back to LINDA*) Now what was I saying? Oh, yes . . .

JOSEPH: (*Interrupting*) I'm sorry to seem awkward, but I'm the only one here. No one else is waiting.

BERNICE: I am very aware of that, sir, or should I call you Mr Smarty Pants? But am I to infer that you have been in this office for two minutes and already you wish to abolish our democratic system of queuing?

JOSEPH: I understand that, but as I'm the only one here, in this case surely it would be a waste of time.

BERNICE: No sir, it would not. Can I remind you that the local government does not invest in these ticket machines for their decorative qualities. The rules state that no one under any circumstances is to be served without a ticket. If I do it for one, the next thing I know, I'll have a riot on my hands. So if you wouldn't mind. (*BERNICE indicates the ticket machine. JOSEPH gives up and walks over to ticket machine under BERNICE's watchful eye. He takes a ticket then sits down*) Thank you, sir. Wasn't too tricky, was it? (*Turns to LINDA*) Right, back to more important matters. There is no nice way of putting it, Lind, except to say that my Leonardo di Caprio* is the most youthful, gorgeous hunk on God's earth, while your Brad Pitt* is an ugly, spiky old twerp!

LINDA: Oh Bernice, you must be blind or stupid. Did you not see him in *Seven*?*

BERNICE: Well, what about Leonardo in *Titanic*?*

LINDA: (*Dreamily*) Oooh Brad in *Legends of the Fall.* *

BERNICE: (*Dreamily*) Leonardo in *What's Eating Gilbert Grape?* * (*Pause, then JOSEPH clears his throat very loudly. BERNICE snaps angrily*) Got a frog in yer throat, have ya? You could do with investing in a pack of Lockets!

LINDA: (*Calming*) Maybe you ought to serve him. I mean, we don't want no complaints, do we?

BERNICE: No, I suppose you're right . . . on this issue. You go over to your desk and I'll sort him out. (*LINDA moves over to other desk*) Number fourteen.

JOSEPH: (*Looks around room as if it were full, then speaks in feigned shock*) Ooh, that must be me. (*He goes over to BERNICE*)

BERNICE: (*Total change in character, she is now overly polite*) Greetings and salutations sir, and how can I be of assistance to you on this glorious morning?

JOSEPH: I'd like to register a birth please.

BERNICE: Certainly. Now, is the young sproglet male or female?

---

* Replace with other actors and films if you wish, as long as they fulfil the necessary criteria!

JOSEPH: Male.

BERNICE: Right, I'll just need to fill out one of these little pink forms. (*In front of her there is a pile of pink forms and a pile of blue forms. She picks up a pink one*)

JOSEPH: Oh sorry, I said male.

BERNICE: (*Confused*) Yes.

JOSEPH: Well, don't you mean you'll need one of these little blue forms?

BERNICE: No sir, as part of our sexual discrimination policy, from now on it's blue forms for the girls and pink forms for the boys. (*She lifts a pink or blue form up each time to demonstrate*)

JOSEPH: Fair enough.

BERNICE: Now, I just need to see if one of our highly busy and fully trained registrars is available to officiate the formalities. (*Looks around room then settles on LINDA*) Ah, Linda, are you currently engaged?

LINDA: Up to my neck in it as always, Bernice, but I'm sure I can facilitate this gentleman.

BERNICE: (*Goes over to LINDA and hands her the form*) Thank you, Linda. He wishes to register a male birth. Here is the (*Deliberately*) pink form.

LINDA: Thank you, Bernice. Won't you take a seat, sir? (*JOSEPH takes a seat opposite LINDA and BERNICE returns to her desk*) Now sir, can you give me the child's surname, please?

JOSEPH: Christ.

LINDA: (*Shocked*) There's no need to swear, sir. This is municipal property. I could have you arrested for using that kind of language.

JOSEPH: Oh no, sorry, you don't understand. Christ is the child's surname. (*Spells it*) C-H-R-I-S-T.

LINDA: Oh I see, well, that's all right then. And his first name or names?

JOSEPH: Jesus.

LINDA: You're off again . . .

JOSEPH: (*Interrupting*) J-E-S-U-S. Jesus is his name.

LINDA: Oh, right. Now your name is?

JOSEPH: Joseph.

LINDA: And your occupation?

JOSEPH: Carpenter.

LINDA: Thank you. And your wife?

JOSEPH: Ah well, you see, she's not, er, well, she's not exactly my wife . . . as in, we're not married, just engaged at present.

LINDA: (*Looking down her nose*) Oh, I see. Well, I'm merely a civil servant, sir, it's not my place to make moral judgements. (*Slight pause*) But I will say this. I don't understand why people can't do things in the right order. Get engaged, get married, have kids – it's simple! It's all gone to pot if you ask me – having kids, then getting married. Really, it wouldn't surprise me if in a few years' time people start filing for divorce before they've even got married. Anyway, where was I? Oh yes, your fiancée's name and occupation.

JOSEPH: Mary, and she is a homemaker.

LINDA: Now which hospital was little Jesus born in, please?

JOSEPH: (*Awkwardly*) Ah, now that is a little bit odd.

LINDA: (*Sarcastic*) Well, you do surprise me, sir.

JOSEPH: You see, he was actually born in a stable.

LINDA: A stable . . . as in amongst straw, gravel and animal poo?

JOSEPH: Yes. You see, that's just the way it was meant to be.

LINDA: Well, I must give you credit sir, that is a noble
            attitude. I know the NHS is a bit stretched, but
            I think if they expected me to give birth in a
            stinky stable, I might have a few words to say on
            the matter. Still, we have it all nowadays, don't
            we? Home births, swimming-pool births . . .
            why not stable births too I say?

JOSEPH: Exactly.

LINDA: Now, before you sign, I just need you to
            double-check the details with me. (*LINDA
            leans across and takes JOSEPH through the
            form*) I've got the birth in a stable covered there.
            Child's full name is Jesus Christ, mother's name
            and occupation is Mary the homemaker, and
            father's name and occupation, Joseph, who is a
            carpenter.

JOSEPH: Ah, one slight discrepancy.

LINDA: Which bit would that be, sir?

JOSEPH: Well . . . the father's name and occupation isn't
            entirely accurate.

LINDA: (*Confused*) Well, that's what you just told me,
            isn't it?

JOSEPH: Yes, but . . . Oh, I don't know how to explain it.

LINDA: (*Losing patience*) Well, come on sir, give it a try.
            What would be a more accurate description of
            the father's name and occupation? Bob the
            postman? Vince the milkman?

JOSEPH: (*Reluctantly*) Well, if you want to be totally
            accurate, I suppose the closest answer would be
            'God, the creator of the universe'.

LINDA: (*Dumbstruck, jaw drops. Pause*) Bernice, can
            you pass me over one of the green forms please?

BERNICE: (*Looks surprised*) Green? Yeah, course. (*Brings
            over green form*)

LINDA: Thank you.

JOSEPH: So, what are the green forms for?
LINDA: Well, we have pink for boys, blue for girls and green for divine appointments.
          (*BERNICE and LINDA both look at JOSEPH who is puzzled. Freeze and blackout*)

TEACHING POINT

The miraculous birth of Jesus is without precedent, and will never be repeated.

BIBLE REFERENCE

Luke 2:1–7

Joseph's Bethlehem Experience

INTRODUCTION

Monologues are most effective as a tool to build on the central things we know about someone's life, and to examine how they may have actually felt.

   I first performed this monologue at a Christmas service in 1996. The greatest compliment I received was from a man who, years before, had been my Sunday school teacher. He told me that through the piece he'd come to a better understanding of Joseph's character, and of how he must have felt when Jesus was born.

Character: JOSEPH.

As the lights come up, JOSEPH enters, singing happily.

JOSEPH: Happiness, happiness, the greatest gift that I possess . . . (*He notices the audience and addresses them*) I'm happy, very happy, incredibly happy. You've probably noticed. But it wasn't always this way. No. A couple of thousand years ago, it was a very different story. I mean, how would you feel? Picture the scene. I'd had a busy day at the carpentry workshop – knocked up a few bookcases, a wardrobe and a couple of mangers. I come home for tea, and the fiancée calls round and tells me she's with child. (*Mimes pregnancy*) Not an everyday occurrence, it has to be said. Now, I admit, I was fairly naïve back then when it came to the old facts of life, but even I knew that holding hands and kissing on a regular basis didn't make a woman pregnant. An explanation was requested, in the nicest possible way, and duly given. Now, I love my Mary more than anyone, so I immediately thought about legally breaking off our engagement to save her from public disgrace and possible stoning. But I must confess, I did find her story about the father's identity a little on the far-fetched side. You probably would have yourself. I mean, I know all about the birds and bees – my mum told me about 'em in graphic detail when I was ten – but all this stuff Mary spun me about angels and heavenly hosts and her having conceived by the Holy Spirit . . . Please, I thought! I reckon that Mary's been on the 'holy spirit' herself, if you catch my drift. (*Mimes swigging from a bottle*)

Forgive me if looking back on it now I seem rather flippant. At the time, I was in the depths of despair. I mean, my Mary, my innocent virgin Mary was pregnant. I feel guilty for thinking some of the things I thought, but come on, with the information available at the time, what would you think? The history books of your ancestors look on me as somewhat insignificant, sort of in the background, only worth a few verses in the Bible. And I don't mind. I mean, I'm not looking for stardom. It would be nice to have a famous actor play me in a film though. I'm always played by some unknown. I've always reckoned I'm a bit Marlon Brando-ish myself. Anyway, what people fail to see is that, at this stage, I was looking at Mary's pregnancy in purely human terms. I knew I hadn't touched her, so the only other possible explanation was Mary had been with another man, and that cut me up bad. It wasn't until I went to bed in a state of shock, to sleep on this revelation, that things took on a more spiritual level.

Now, I don't know if any of you have ever been visited by an angel. Well, it was my first time. 'Do not be afraid,' he said. 'Take Mary home as your wife. What she has conceived is of the Holy Spirit. Your son will save the people from their sins.' Mind-blowing stuff, eh? But my first feeling, when all this had sunk in, was relief. Pure relief that my Mary was telling the truth, innocence intact. Then it was total joy at the great privilege given to us, to bring God's own son into this world. Absolutely cosmic!

So, if you ever think your feelings go up and down a bit, remember the story of Joseph's emotional roller coaster, from despair to relief and joy in one fell swoop! The Bethlehem experience has been life-changing for me. I hope it is for you. Don't let it pass you by as 'just a nice story'. Believe me, there's a lot more to it than that. I was upset about one thing though: I had hoped to call our first child something in the more modern line. Damon or Farquhar. But under the circumstances, we were happy to do what the prophets had foretold. So, in our makeshift maternity ward, all those years ago, we named our first son – Jesus. (*Fade to blackout*)

TEACHING POINT

To give an insight into the human impact of Jesus' birth, through the eyes of his earthly father.

BIBLE REFERENCE

Matthew 1:18–25

Paparazzi!

INTRODUCTION

This monologue looks at the birth of Christ through the eyes of a paparazzo journalist. The majority of the piece is spoken directly to the audience and takes place soon after the nativity.

Character: CHRISTOPHER, a member of the paparazzi.

CHRISTOPHER enters looking flustered, with a camera around his neck, holding a portfolio. He throws the portfolio on the floor and some nativity pictures fall out.

CHRIS: (*To himself*) All the way from the city I came to cover this story. 'Go on, Christopher,' they say. 'It's a royal birth, a once-in-a-lifetime opportunity.' I might've known something was fishy when they said it was in Bethlehem. They must think my aftershave is eau de dung, all the ploppy old jobs they give me.

(*Notices audience and addresses them*) Oh, do excuse me. Please allow me to introduce myself, ladies and gentlemen. Christopher St John Smythe's the name, freelance photographer for *The Judea Chronicle*, also available for weddings, graduations and the odd glamour shoot. (*Hands out business cards to audience*) Reasonable rates, of course. Currently residing in the entertainment capital of Eastern civilisation – Bethlehem!

Why Bethlehem? I hear you ask. And well you may ask. To cover a royal birth. And I can tell you, it's been a real eye-opener from the beginning. When I first arrived in town, I thought I'd check into a posh hotel – you know, the ones with the monogrammed towels and duck feather pillows. Wrong! No one in Bethlehem had even heard of a hotel, much less owned one. One of the townsfolk informed me, 'You'll 'ave to find an inn, but they're prob'ly all filled up 'cos of the census!' Well, can you imagine me, Christopher St John Smythe, residing in an inn? A joke! Still, given few options, I eventually found one owned by a snaggle-toothed old hag who agreed to take me in. (*Change voice*) 'Oh yes, my dear, I'll squeeze you in. I always feel a bit sorry for you bald and ugly ones. I see you've got a camera there. Maybe you can take a few sexy shots of me, in lieu of payment.' I was left with little or no choice. So, after I'd settled in to my cupboard under the stairs, I decided to venture out into Bethlehem to find the royal palace. I was expecting a welcoming committee for the world's press, with a generous spread of champagne and prawn vindaloo vol au vents. How wrong could I have been! I was to find that Bethlehem has no royal palace, no royalty, not even a duke! Just lots and lots and lots of inns . . . and smelly stables. No, I wasn't to find myself surrounded by kingly robes walking on polished marble floors in a royal palace, but instead I was stuck with a selection of the most revolting farmyard animals, knee-deep in animal poo in a ramshackle stable. Still, it was a lesson in humility and no mistake.

The alleged 'royal birth' was an interesting departure from what I had expected. The parents proudly looked down on their baby, and I must admit they did have an endearing innocent charm about them. Mary and Joseph invited me into the stable, along with some shepherds, who had very originally brought gifts of sheep. They were full of some extraordinary story about angelic choirs giving a concert on the hillside, or something. Haven't got time to check out their story. They seemed genuine enough, but of course, simple country folk like that can be very gullible.

Mary smiled at me and asked if I would like to hold the child. I did. I cradled him in my arms and I felt a real warmth. He'd wet himself down the front of my brand new Yves St Laurent shirt! As I laid the baby back in the manger, our eyes met, and I had the distinct feeling that this was no ordinary baby. I felt he had great insight and would grow up to be a remarkable young man.

Mary and Joseph, being from out in the sticks, had never seen a camera before, so asked if I would show them what it did. So I took a series of photographs. I've got them here. (*He picks up some classic Christmas card pictures from the portfolio on the floor*) They're not bad. You never know, they may become classics. All in all, I feel my trip to Bethlehem has been worthwhile, even though it wasn't exactly a royal birth. Unfortunately, a child born in a stable is just another sign of the times. Personally, I blame the Tories. Don't suppose any of this will be remembered in five or ten years' time, will it? Yet somehow I feel good about myself, uplifted. Call me sentimental, but this poor young family has really touched me. I'm not a religious man, although I do believe in God of course, but holding that baby was the nearest thing to a spiritual experience I can remember. (*Wistful*) Almost like God was trying to get a message through to me . . . (*Matter-of-fact, jokey again*) Anyway, enough of all this – must dash back to Judea. Just had some hot gossip that some celebrity stargazers are heading for Herod's palace. (*Starts to leave*) Could be a great photo-story, so I'm off to get the exclusive. (*Exit and blackout*)

TEACHING POINT

The wonder of the nativity story is for everyone, whoever they are.

BIBLE REFERENCE

Luke 2:8–20

Einstein, Freud and Newton's Theory of Astrology

INTRODUCTION

I wrote this piece originally for a Christmas service, to lead into a song by Graham Kendrick called 'Seekers and dreamers'. The sketch begins by taking a humorous look at the three wise men in Harrods, buying their gifts for Jesus. It ends with them reflecting that maybe it is not them seeking the Messiah, but rather the Messiah seeking them.

Characters: EINSTEIN; FREUD; NEWTON.

On stage there are three beautifully decorated tables with a gift on each. As the sketch develops, the gifts are revealed as gold, frankincense and myrrh. EINSTEIN, FREUD and NEWTON enter and walk to centre stage looking around.

EINSTEIN: What did you say this place was called, Freud?
FREUD: Harrods.
EINSTEIN: Good, is it?
FREUD: Apparently so.
EINSTEIN: Well, it's big enough anyway. We must be able to find something suitable. What are you going to get him, Newton?
NEWTON: I don't know yet, but when I see it, I've got this feeling I'll know straight away. What about you?

245

EINSTEIN: No idea! Oh look, what about a nice set of talking Teletubbies?*

FREUD: Don't be so ridiculous, Einstein.

EINSTEIN: What! There's nothing wrong with Tinky-Winky, Dipsy, Laa-Laa and Po!?* You've got to get him something that's modern.

FREUD: Yes, but the Teletubbies* will be out of date in five minutes.

EINSTEIN: All right, how about a lovely pair of Thomas the Tank Engine pyjamas then? Thomas never goes out of fashion. (*FREUD sighs. NEWTON has spotted one of the tables*)

NEWTON: (*Picks up gift*) Hey, I think I've found something.

EINSTEIN: Oh yeah – what you got?

NEWTON: Myrrh.

EINSTEIN: Myrrh! What's that then?

FREUD: Are you thick or something, Einstein?

EINSTEIN: Come on then Freud, if you're so clever, what is it?

FREUD: Well, it's . . . it's . . . I dunno. What is it, Newton?

EINSTEIN: Ahhh!

NEWTON: It's a kind of aromatic spice.

EINSTEIN: Oh, has she replaced Ginger° then?

NEWTON: What?

EINSTEIN: Aromatic Spice . . . Baby, Posh, Scary, Sporty and now Aromatic.°

NEWTON: It's nothing to do with the Spice Girls,° dopey! It's an actual spice, quite rare too. (*FREUD goes over to second gift*)

---

* Replace with more contemporary toy as necessary.

° Replace with more appropriate topical reference as necessary.

EINSTEIN: (*Sarcastic*) Oh, very exciting. I'm sure the baby Messiah will jump for joy!

NEWTON: I couldn't care less if you like it or not, it's what I'm going to give him.

EINSTEIN: Whatever . . . if you insist. (*Sniffs air*) Here, what's that pong?

FREUD: (*Brings over gift*) I think it's this. (*Hands gift to EINSTEIN*)

EINSTEIN: Eeuucchh! What's that?

FREUD: Frankincense.

EINSTEIN: Frankenstein! Smells like his decomposing remains. (*Hands gift back*)

FREUD: Not Frankenstein, Einstein. Frankincense. It's a kind of perfume or incense.

EINSTEIN: Frankincense and myrrh. For a pair of supposedly wise men, you two are certainly lacking in the brains department.

NEWTON: Well, come on then, if you're so wonderful, what are you going to take him?

EINSTEIN: I don't know. I can't seem to find anything that quite takes my . . . (*He stops suddenly as he spots the third gift. As he stops we hear a 'Ding!' (ringing) sound, the sound of sudden inspiration*) Hello, what's this then? (*He goes to gift*) Wow!

NEWTON: What is it?

EINSTEIN: A twenty-four-carat gold Winnie the Pooh! This I've got to get.

FREUD: There we are, all sorted! I think our gifts have got quite a nice ring to them. Gold, frankincense and myrrh.

EINSTEIN: Not bad at all, Freud. Come on, let's pay up, then get back on the trail of our star.

NEWTON: You know, I've been thinking about this star a lot. We've been following it for thousands of miles, but what if it's a never-ending quest? I mean, if you think about it, we're risking everything on one star.

EINSTEIN: Yes, but what a wonderful one to risk it on! I've been studying stars nearly all my life, reading them and analysing them. And I can honestly say, I've never been 100 per cent sure of any of my findings – until now. When I look at that star, I know; I really know we've got it right. This is no wild goose chase.

FREUD: Do you think it's really us that's doing the seeking then?

EINSTEIN: What do you mean?

FREUD: Well, following this star seems too easy, doesn't it? I've started to think, maybe it's not us that's seeking him so much, but rather him seeking us, using the star to guide us home. Just a thought.

EINSTEIN: (*Pause*) I hate to admit it, Freud, but you could just be right. Still, there's only one way to find out. Come on, let's go. (*They all exit. Fade to blackout*)

TEACHING POINT

Jesus is seeking for us to seek after him.

BIBLE REFERENCE

Matthew 2:1–12

Christmas Rapping

INTRODUCTION

This is a great piece for a group of keen and talented children to do to really spark up any Christmas service or presentation. A short sketch leads into a rapped performance of 'Away in a Manger'. Don't be put off by the necessary rehearsal for this one; it's not as bad as you might think, and the end result is definitely worth it. A group of fantastic kids rapped 'Away in a Manger' at my church one Christmas and stole the show.

Characters: Four children; OLD LADY; OLD MAN.

The Four children all enter wrapped in winter coats/blankets etc. They are holding carol song-sheets and a portable stereo system.

ONE: How much have we got so far then?

TWO: (*Counting*) Um . . . one, twenty, forty . . . six . . . £1.68.

THREE: (*Depressed*) Not much, is it? Three hours solid we've been at it. It's hardly worth the bother for fifty pence an hour.

FOUR: Fifty-six pence an hour to be precise. Fourteen pence an hour each times three . . . that's forty-two pence each.

THREE: Forty-two pence – pathetic. Pathetic. We might just as well pack it in.

ONE: Come on, chin up. We're making a stand here for a new style of carol singing, remember!

TWO: Yeah, it's not just the money, it's the pride.

THREE: Come on then. You lot sound more like adults every day. (*A slight pause, then THREE nudges FOUR*) Are you gonna knock on the door then, brains?

FOUR: (*Mimes knocking door*) Knock knock.

OLD LADY: (*Calling from offstage*) Who's there?

ONE: Carol singers.

OLD LADY: Carol singers who?

THREE: (*Impatiently*) Carol singers who wanna earn some money. Now open up, you silly . . . (*tails off as TWO puts his hand over THREE's mouth*)

TWO: Ssshhhh! We're just four harmless young children who are singing carols to earn a few pence.

THREE: (*Pushes hand away and calls*) Pounds! (*TWO quickly puts his hand back over THREE's mouth*)

OLD LADY: Ooh, hold on, I'll just get my husband.
(*Pause while OLD LADY gets OLD MAN to come to the door. During this TWO and THREE start bickering while ONE and FOUR try to stop them. The old couple come to the door*)

OLD LADY: Oh, look at the little precious darlings, all nicely wrapped up against the cold. Don't they look sweet, Herbert?

OLD MAN: Yeah!

OLD LADY: When I was a young girl . . .

THREE: (*Despairing*) Oh no! (*TWO and FOUR elbow him in the ribs from either side*)

OLD LADY: (*Ignoring them*) Yes, when I was a young girl,

I used to go carol singing at Christmas and if we were lucky we'd get a shiny sixpence to put in the Christmas pudding, wouldn't we, Herbert?

OLD MAN: Yeah!

ONE: Is there any particular carol you'd like us to sing?

OLD LADY: Oh yes. 'Away in a Manger', please. Always been my favourite, hasn't it, Herbert?

OLD MAN: Yeah!

ONE: OK, 'Away in a Manger' it is. (*They stand in a huddle and begin to sing 'Away in a Manger' in traditional out-of-tune style for one verse*)

THREE: (*Interrupts suddenly*) Kick it! (*As he says this, TWO presses play on the stereo and they all tear off overcoats to reveal trendy rappers' gear and put on a pair of dark glasses. Either through the stereo, or controlled through a separate sound system, play a rap backing track to which the children rap along the lyrics of 'Away in a Manger'. This will obviously take a bit of rehearsal, but it is great fun and the kids will love it! If possible, as well as sharing out the lyrics, work out a basic movement routine. It doesn't have to be a choreographed work of art; something very basic serves the purpose. During the rap, the old couple join in the movement and possibly even take a section of the rap. It is important that the OLD MAN only ever says 'Yeah' – which isn't very difficult during a rap! As an alternative to a backing track, you could forget the stereo and create a beat-box effect vocally. This would be done by all the cast not rapping at the time. Make sure the piece has an obvious ending rather than just tailing off*)

ONE: (*To OLD LADY*) Did you enjoy it?

OLD LADY: Oh yes, it was wicked! (*She gives them some money*) There you are, and I hope you have a very happy Christmas.

ONE/TWO
THREE/FOUR: (*Together*) Thanks, bye. (*They all collect gear and exit*)

OLD LADY: Jolly good, weren't they, Herbert?

OLD MAN: (*Short pause*) Yeah! (*Freeze and blackout*)

TEACHING POINT

Rather than trying to put across a particular teaching point, this sketch gives a modern slant on the Christmas story and would need to be accompanied by a short talk.

BIBLE REFERENCE

Luke 2:1–7

The Unwanted Christmas Present

INTRODUCTION

In the millennium era, it is so important that our children understand who Jesus is. This sketch highlights the problem that so many people have no idea who he is, or what he stands for. Children will absolutely love this sketch, particularly as its most important element is that the children are all played by adults! It will be important for the ensemble during rehearsal to really read between the lines and work on childish reactions and mannerisms.

Characters: DAVE; SOPHIE; RACHEL; ANDY: brothers and sisters aged five to seven.

It is Christmas Eve and the characters are getting excited at the prospect of Santa and Christmas presents. The four of them share duvets on the floor. As the lights go up, DAVE is at the front of the stage keeping a lookout for Mum and Dad. Much to his annoyance, the other three, who are pretending to be asleep, start laughing.

DAVE:	Shut up, right, and I'll tell you something. (*All kneel up on duvets*)
SOPHIE:	What?
RACHEL:	What?
ANDY:	What?
DAVE:	I saw Mummy and Daddy, right, having a right long snog underneath the holly. (*He leaps up in excitement*)

253

SOP/RAC/AND: (*Together*) Mistletoe! (*All start laughing. DAVE shows off and pretends he's wet himself. The other three start to chant*) David's gone and wet himself. (*Repeat, getting faster*)

DAVE: (*Interrupting*) Not really! Anyway, you lot better shut up or I'll tell Mummy and she'll tell Santa and he won't leave you any pressies.

SOPHIE: Well I want Santa to leave me a Boyzone* cassette 'cos I love Ronan.

RACHEL: Well I want Santa to leave me a Boyzone poster 'cos I love Steve.

ANDY: Well I want Santa to leave me a Boyzone lunchbox 'cos I love Mikey.

DAV/SOP/RAC: (*Together*) Uuggghhhh!

ANDY: (*Indignant*) What?

SOPHIE: You're not allowed to love Mikey 'cos you're a boy!

ANDY: Well, I'm gonna be Mikey in the show for Mummy and Daddy tomorrow.

ALL: (*Together*) The show!

RACHEL: We'd better rehearse or we'll all go wrong.

ALL: Yeah! (*They line up and perform part of a Boyzone number. At the end of the number ANDY attempts the splits, which goes painfully wrong*)

ANDY: Aaagh! (*SOPHIE and RACHEL help ANDY who is in pain*)

DAVE: (*Manically rushes around stage*) Sshhhh! Sshhhh! Mummy's coming, Mummy's

---

* Replace throughout as necessary.

coming! (*SOPHIE, RACHEL and ANDY settle in bed and pretend they are snoring. DAVE waits till they have settled, smiles and tiptoes to the head of the other three*) Not really!

SOP/RAC/AND: (*Together*) Oh David!

DAVE: Look you lot, you'd better shut up or I won't tell you a secret.

SOPHIE: (*Crawling up to DAVE*) Oh go on . . . Please!

RACHEL: (*Crawling up to DAVE*) Pleeaasseeee!

ANDY: (*Crawling up to DAVE*) Plleeeaaasssseeee! (*They all continue to beg as DAVE indignantly shakes his head*)

DAVE: (*Eventually*) Oh OK. I know where the pressies are, and what we've all got.

SOPHIE: What have I got?

RACHEL: What have I got?

ANDY: What have I got?

DAVE: Not telling ya.

SOPHIE: Oh go on, please.

RACHEL: Please.

ANDY: Please! (*DAVE shakes his head as they continue begging*)

RACHEL: (*Confidently*) Well, I know what the best present is anyway 'cos my teacher told me!

DAVE: (*Pause*) What?

RACHEL: Jesus.

ANDY: What's he got to do with Christmas?

DAV/SOP/RAC: (*Together*) Don't you know? (*They all take the mickey*)

SOPHIE: Well, right, Joseph and his amazing technicolour dreamcoat took Mary to Bethlehem to have a baby.

DAVE: Yeah, and it was so long ago Jason Donovan was Joseph and not Phillip Schofield.

RACHEL: They looked around everywhere to find somewhere to have the baby, but all they could find was a horrible smelly stable . . .

SOPHIE: So Mary had the baby and wrapped him in . . . um . . . Joseph's rainbow coat, and there were shepherds, wise men, angels and a big star.

RACHEL: And that's why we have a star on the top of the Christmas tree.

DAVE: (*Pause. With a cheeky grin, he produces a Christmas tree star*) Not any more, we haven't. I swapped it for your Boyzone Steve doll! (*DAVE, SOPHIE and ANDY all laugh. RACHEL looks upset*)

RACHEL: Oh, well look! We shouldn't be thinking about Boyzone. We should be thinking about Jesus. It is his birthday, after all.

DAVE: (*Pause*) Well, let's have a vote on it. Hands up for Christmas with pressies, food and a Boyzone Christmas show. (*DAVE, SOPHIE and ANDY eagerly throw up their hands*)

SOPHIE: And hands up for Christmas with Jesus in the stable with the smelly animals. (*RACHEL puts her hand up*)

DAV/SOP/AND: (*Mocking RACHEL*) Na na na na na.

DAVE: (*Calms down*) Look, shut up, you lot. Do you wanna know where the pressies are or not?

SOPHIE: Do you really know?

RACHEL: Do you really, really know?

ANDY: Do you really, really, really, really know?

DAVE: Yeah. They're in Mum's wardrobe. Come
                 on, I'll show ya. (*DAVE tiptoes round the
                 bedroom then stands crouched near back
                 of stage facing audience. The others follow
                 him and create a chain*) Are you ready?
                 (*They nod and then creep along looking to
                 either side and humming creepily, 'Dum
                 dum dum dum dum, dum dum dum dum'*)

SOPHIE: Mummy's coming. (*They all look panic-
                 stricken and run back to bed. DAVE runs
                 around bedroom manically before he joins
                 the others under the duvet. They all
                 pretend to snore. After a short pause,
                 SOPHIE pops up, smiling*)

SOPHIE: Not really. (*The others groan. Blackout*)

TEACHING POINT

The importance of teaching our children the truth about
Jesus.

BIBLE REFERENCES

Matthew 18:10–14; 2 Timothy 3:15

Christmas with Lizzie

INTRODUCTION

This is a great sketch to add humour to any Christmas service or presentation. The piece gives the actors an opportunity for some really over-the-top caricature performances, especially the actor playing Del. The underlying message exposes the widely held view that being British, thus belonging to a so-called Christian nation, automatically makes you a Christian. It will stand equally well on its own, or with a talk looking at what makes a person truly Christian.

Characters: DEL, loud-mouthed yobbish father; MAUREEN, his long-suffering wife; LISA, his precocious teenage daughter; MIKEY, his five-year-old son; GRAN, his mother who has totally lost her marbles.

The lights go up on Del and Maureen's front room. It's three o'clock on Christmas Day and boredom has set in. DEL is asleep on the sofa. MAUREEN is offstage in the kitchen. LISA is listening to her Walkman. GRAN is dozing in the armchair. MIKEY is playing with a car on the floor.

	(*DEL snores loudly*)
MAUREEN:	(*Offstage*) Oh no, Del! The flippin' oven's playing up.
MIKEY:	(*Loudly and nudging DEL*) Dad! Dad! The batteries have run out. Can you fix it, Dad?
GRAN:	(*Singing out of tune*) 'The hills are alive with the sound of music . . .'

258

LISA: (*Having a rave with her headphones on*) No . . . No . . . There's no limits. (*or any current song*) (*Cast all repeat together a few times causing a cacophony of sound*)

DEL: (*Jumps up suddenly and shouts*) Stop! (*All cast freeze in silence*) It's three o'clock. We're missing the Queen's speech. (*He rushes to the front of centre stage and switches on TV. Sits back down staring at TV*) Love! It's the Queen's speech. Hurry up!

MAUREEN: (*Offstage*) What d'ya say, love?

DEL: Hurry up, woman! Yer missing Lizzie's speech!

MAUREEN: (*Shimmies in and sits next to DEL on sofa*) What she said so far then? Anything about all the homeless? (*DEL looks at her in impatient disbelief*) Oh, it's so sad. And those Bosnians and the Wandenese. Ooh, and what about her Charles?

DEL: Why don't you shut your trap, woman? She ain't said nuffin' yet, and what wiv all your gassing, we're missing it!

LISA: Dad . . . (*DEL ignores her, so she shouts*) Dad!

DEL: (*Irritably*) What?

LISA: Can I watch the Boyzone* Christmas Special at four o'clock? It's got a profile of Ronan and Steve, and I love Ronan.

DEL: No, you flamin' can't!

LISA: (*Whingeing*) Oh, why?

DEL: 'Cos as I've told you before, young lady, they've got a re-run of the 1976 *Morecambe and Wise Christmas Special* on the other channel. Now,

---

* Replace as necessary.

can we have a bit of peace and quiet for Her Majesty? Our monarch, our ruler.

MAUREEN: Oh, come on Del. Calm down a bit, won't ya? She's only human like us!

LISA: Yeah!

DEL: (*Sarcastically*) Only human. Like you two! Do me a favour, won't ya! (*To MAUREEN*) Does the Queen dye her hair every fortnight? Does Her Majesty do herself up like some nineteen-year-old, in a stupid bid to regain her long-lost youth? (*To LISA*) Does the Queen dream about running off into the sunset with some bloke out of a *Boys' Own** comic? No, I don't think she does, does she? So can we all shut up and listen (*Shouts*) before I go nuts! (*Pause and stunned silence*)

MIKEY: Dad, can you put some new batteries in my car?

DEL: (*Irate*) No! (*MIKEY starts whimpering and DEL slaps him round the head*)

GRAN: (*Sings National Anthem to indicate end of speech*) 'God save our gracious Queen'. . . (*As she sings, DEL proudly rises, stands still then marches to the TV as the song ends and then switches it off*)

DEL: Oh, good speech that, wonderful speech. Wonderful example of true royalty. Not one of those hanger-onners. Blue blood that lady's got pumping through her veins, royal blue blood. Great advert for our Christian faith.

MAUREEN: (*Stares at DEL in disbelief*) What do you

---

* Replace as necessary.

	know about Christianity?
LISA:	Yeah!
DEL:	(*Defensively*) I know a lot about Christianity, thank you very much. Only been a Christian all my life! Been a regular church-goer all my life too – every Christmas, every Easter. Well, except this year of course, but you know the trouble I've had with my prostate. (*Pulls a face and shifts uncomfortably*)
MIKEY:	Dad, can I be a Christian too?
DEL:	You are one, my boy! You're British through and through, not one of these foreigners littering up the country. As long as you're British, go to church regular, and follow the example of the Queen, then you're a Christian. (*Pause. DEL settles back then suddenly sees time and jumps up*) Oh no! It's four o'clock. We're missing the *Morecambe and Wise Christmas Special*. (*Rushes to switch on TV again and sits back down*)
ALL:	(*Whole cast stare at TV and start singing Morecambe and Wise theme tune*) 'Bring me sunshine, in your smile . . .' (*GRAN starts singing her out-of-tune 'Sound of Music' over the top. Lights fade to blackout*)

TEACHING POINT

Only those who believe in Jesus Christ are truly Christian, regardless of their nationality, upbringing, church attendance, good deeds or age.

BIBLE REFERENCES

Matthew 7:21; John 3:16

The Bloggs' Christmas

INTRODUCTION

The Bloggs family are making their Christmas preparations, during which they have a discussion on the central point of Christmas. Master Bloggs, as usual, is 'defender of the faith'. As with all the Bloggs sketches, go for strong caricature and lots of laughs!

Characters: MR BLOGGS; MRS BLOGGS; MASTER BLOGGS; MISS BLOGGS.

Lights go up on the Bloggs family who are all seated. MR BLOGGS is sorting through a box of decorations, MRS BLOGGS is reading the Radio Times, *MASTER BLOGGS is wrapping gifts and MISS BLOGGS is looking through a large box of cards.*

MR:	(*Lifts up tangled set of tree lights*) Oh, stone me! Who put these lights away last year? It looks like they're in a reef knot!
MISS:	Well, it weren't me.
MASTER:	Nor me.
MRS:	Don't look at me!
MR:	What, they magically put themselves away on their own, did they?
MRS:	No, you put 'em away.
MR:	I did not!
MRS:	Yes, you did, Mr Bloggs, I vividly remember it. I said to you, 'You'll regret it next Christmas if you just shove 'em in that box willy nilly,' but you told

262

me to get lost and mind my own business!

MR: Well, I don't recall that. (*Picks bent angel out of box*) Oh look at the state of that angel!

MASTER: (*Wrapping gift*) Pass us the sellotape please, Miss Bloggs. (*She throws it over*) And the scissors. (*She also throws them over*)

MR: Mind out with that lot, will you! You'll take someone's eye out in a minute!

MISS: They're safety scissors, Mr Bloggs.

MR: Well, you're still not supposed to chuck 'em about all over the shop!

MRS: Ooh look, they've got that *Braveheart* on BBC 1 Christmas Eve . . . ooh, Mel Gibson . . .

MISS: Ooh, he's gorgeous ain't he, Mrs Bloggs?

MRS: Mmmm.

MR: Not a patch on me though, eh? (*MRS and MISS BLOGGS laugh*) Ahhh, you can laugh . . .

MASTER: Any other good films on then, Mrs Bloggs?

MRS: Oh, just the usual, Master Bloggs. *The Sound of Music*.

MISS: *Mary Poppins*.

MR: *Indiana Jones* – and the two hours of doom!

MASTER: What about James Bond?

MRS: Of course! What would Christmas afternoon be like without the Bond film?

MR: Which one is it?

MRS: *You Only Live Twice*.

MR: Is that Roger Moore or Sean Connery?

MRS: Er . . . ooh, Sean Connery!

MISS: Ooh, he's gorgeous, ain't he, Mrs Bloggs?

MRS: Mmmm.

MR: All right, all right. I think we've had enough of you two lusting for one afternoon!

MASTER: Chuck us over a decent Christmas card from that box, Miss Bloggs.

MISS: Out of this box? You'll be lucky, they're all naff!

MRS: Oi! Don't be so cheeky, Miss Bloggs. I bought them.

MISS: Well, I don't know why.

MRS: You know exactly why. 'Cos they was cheap! Hundred in the box for ninety-nine pence!

MISS: Yeah, but look at 'em! They've all got candles and baubles and bells on 'em. And then there's twelve religious ones in the box – twelve! I don't know why they have to go overboard on religion just 'cos it's Christmas.

MASTER: (*Shocked*) What?

MR: Don't worry, Miss Bloggs, we'll send the manky ones with the baubles and bells to the obscure aunts and uncles we don't like, ha ha ha!

MASTER: (*Still in shock*) I can't believe you just said that.

MR: Well, we never see 'em from one year to the next!

MASTER: Not you, Mr Bloggs. Miss Bloggs.

MISS: What did I say?

MASTER: That you don't know why they go overboard on religion just 'cos it's Christmas.

MISS: Well, they do!

MRS: It's true, Master Bloggs, they do tend to go a bit mad.

MASTER: Oh, for goodness' sake. What's the central point of Christmas?

MR: Food! Turkeys, dates, chocolate logs, nuts and cheese footballs.

MISS: Pressies! Socks, hankies, talcum powder, CDs, make-up, clothes. Play Stations, bicycles and home entertainment systems.

MR: Ha! You'll be lucky.

MRS: Oh, listen to you two shallow idiots. Food and pressies, I ask you. It's television, innit? The Queen's speech, *Only Fools and Horses*, *One*

Foot in the Grave, Morecambe and Wise re-runs and *Jim Davidson's Generation Game*.

MR: Jim Davidson! He's not a patch on our Brucey. (*Mimics Bruce Forsyth*) Nice to see you, to see you . . . (*Others join in with 'Nice!'*)

MASTER: Hang on a minute! You're all missing the whole point of it. Christmas isn't an excuse to eat, drink, get presents and watch naff telly. It's supposed to be a celebration of the birth of Christ, and that's why they (*Mimics MISS BLOGGS*) 'go overboard on religion'.

MISS: Well, you would say that, wouldn't you, 'cos you're all religious.

MASTER: It's got nothing to do with me being religious, Miss Bloggs. Whether you're Christian, Muslim or a complete atheist, it doesn't alter the historical fact that the Christmas festival is the celebration of the birth of God's Son, does it?

MRS: So, you don't think we should eat, drink and watch telly then, Master Bloggs?

MASTER: I'm not saying that at all. Those things are all fine in their place, as long as we don't completely forget the true meaning of Christmas.

MRS: Well, I suppose so. What do you think, Mr Bloggs?

MR: (*Pause for thought*) Pass us the nuts. (*Fade to blackout*)

TEACHING POINT

The razzmatazz of Christmas may be enjoyable, but it is ultimately meaningless unless Jesus Christ is at the heart of the celebrations.

BIBLE REFERENCE

Luke 2:1–7

Reference Section

Category Index

For easy reference, the titles of the sketches in each category are listed, followed by the page number in brackets.

Monologues

These should be well rehearsed and performed by a strong actor.

Two-handers

These sketches can be performed with two actors. Most can be easily adapted to suit your ratio of male/female performers.

Narrated

In these sketches, most or all of the lines are delivered by a narrator or narrators. Some are particularly useful if rehearsal time is minimal.
Sermon on Mount Wembley (77); Clever Trevor and Thick Nick (81, needs CHORUS); Old Mac Jethro (84, needs ENSEMBLE to sing); Do the Same (89); The Prodigal (98); A Nice Slice of Talent (112); Who Am I? (198).

Raps/Rhymes

These pieces will need quite a lot of rehearsal to produce the best effect.
Clever Trevor and Thick Nick (81); Old Mac Jethro (84); Christmas Rapping (249).

Encouraging creativity

Lots of scope here for the group to come up with ideas of their own, giving the piece their own individual style.
Destination Tel Aviv (62); Sermon on Mount Wembley (77); Clever Trevor and Thick Nick (81); Old Mac Jethro (84); Do the Same (89); Ask, Seek, Knock (94); The Prodigal (98); A Nice Slice of Talent (112); Loadsalove (168); Who Am I? (198); The Titch and the Tree (213); Christmas Rapping (249).

Suitable for children

These are the sketches which are most suitable for use with younger children, either to work towards a performance, or simply as learn-by-doing exercises.
Sermon on Mount Wembley (77); Clever Trevor and Thick Nick (81); Old Mac Jethro (84); Do the Same (89); The Prodigal (98); Christmas Rapping (249).

Prior knowledge needed

These sketches need only a very basic knowledge of Scripture, but it is worth bearing in mind who your audience will be before performing them. Alternatively, the sketch could be linked with some form of teaching which sets the scene.

Dirty Water (46); Hole in the Roof (51); Bric-à-Brac Jack (72); Five Hundred Excuses (103); Kiss of Death (118); The Last Temptation (122); Final Requests (126); Beef Stew Without Dumplings (140); The Titch and the Tree (213); The Registrar (230); Joseph's Bethlehem Experience (237).

Suitable for schools

A difficult list to keep short, as most of the sketches are suitable for use in schools, depending on the age group of the audience, and actors available to perform. Look at the following as a starting-point.

Feeding the Five Million (59); Destination Tel Aviv (62); Sermon on Mount Wembley (77); Clever Trevor and Thick Nick (81); Old Mac Jethro (84); Do the Same (89); The Prodigal (98); A Nice Slice of Talent (112); The Why Files (129); Alternative Lord's Prayer (144); Kids' Talk (158); Who Am I? (198); Calendar System (203); Millennium Party (206); The Titch and the Tree (213); Christmas Rapping (249); The Unwanted Christmas Present (253); The Bloggs' Christmas (262).

Subject Index

273

Scripture Index

Mark

Luke

John

1 Corinthians

Galatians

Ephesians

2 Timothy

25 Sketches About Proverbs

by David Burt

A hen-pecked husband camps on his own roof for 16 years; Charles and Jennifer prepare for the end of the world; Adam and Eve hide apple cores from God; Ulysses the unicorn turns down a ride with Noah; the disciples argue over a tube of Pringles.

The book of Proverbs in the Bible has long been a source of wit and wisdom for people of various ages, races and cultures. So what better resource could we have for creating funny but poignant sketches about everyday life?

From subjects as diverse as betrayal, bullying, laziness and loneliness, there is something here for everyone!

Ideal for seeker-friendly services and all-age worship.

100 Instant Discussion Starters

by John Buckeridge

100 'strange but true' stories will get any group
thinking, laughing, possibly outraged – but definitely
talking!

- Fully indexed by themes and Bible references
  for ease of use.
- Questions and 'application' sections, follow
  each anecdote, plus an extensive list of Bible
  references to lead into a group study.
- Includes guidance on how to run discussion
  groups.
- Excellent resource for cells or 'after Alpha'
  groups.
- Useful source of material for talks and sermons
  as well!

50 Easy Outreach Ideas

by Paul Mogford

You've heard of friendship evangelism – but between earning a living, spending time with the family and church meetings, what time is there for making new friends?

These easy outreach events are designed to be organised with the minimum of fuss for maximum fun and friendship!

From the humble church picnic to a jazz or jive evening, it's all here – all you have to do is open your heart, then open the book.